Parkinson's Lore

When I was born my paternal grandmother
tried very hard to have me called Melbourne
because MCC had just won a test match there.
Fortunately my mother, a southerner of great
common sense, would have none of it. Not so
my father who, being a Yorkshireman and
therefore cricket mad, was torn between Herbert
(Sutcliffe), Percy (Holmes) or Hedley (Verity).
Mother, fortunately, settled for Michael and
would not budge. That was the only concession
my old man made during the next twenty years
which he devoted to producing a son who
would one day play for Yorkshire.

PARKINSON'S LORE

Michael Parkinson

with drawings by Michael Lewis

ARROW BOOKS

Most of these pieces originally appeared in
The Sunday Times and *Punch,* and the author
gratefully acknowledges the editors for their
permission to reproduce the pieces in this form.

Arrow Books Limited
17–21 Conway Street, London W1P 6JD

An imprint of the Hutchinson Publishing Group

London Melbourne Sydney Auckland
Johannesburg and agencies
throughout the world

First published by Pavilion Books
in association with Michael Joseph 1981
Arrow edition 1982

Made and printed in Great Britain
by The Anchor Press Ltd
Tiptree, Essex

ISBN 0 09 928360 3

Parkinson's Lore

I was born in a council house in the Yorkshire mining village of Cudworth on a housing estate nicknamed 'Debtors' Retreat', where the rent collectors walked in pairs. As a kid growing up there it helped if you could either fight or run. I was a runner.

I liked the place. It was ragged-arsed, snotty-nosed and ugly, but it was never boring. It had four or five Nonconformist chapels, six or seven boozers and one cinema which became the focal point of my life. It was called The Rock for reasons which had something to do with the seats, and it was here that I fell in love with Joan Leslie and Cyd Charisse who were confections of the Dream Factory, and Pat Heaton and Mavis Lodge, who were not, but whom I never got to sit with on the back row.

I spent the greater part of my childhood in the cinema. I went every Sunday, Monday, Wednesday and Friday, which was when they changed the programmes. If I didn't turn up they used to send someone down to our house to find out what was wrong. In what passed for the cultural society of Cudworth, going to the pictures was better than wasting your money at the boozer – but not as uplifting as going to chapel and listening to the Messiah.

Every one of the chapels used to produce its version of the Messiah each year and it seemed to me that the work was in production for 10 months out of the 12 in our village. I had a friend whose family were keen chapel-goers and Messiah addicts and, once a year, I'd be scrubbed until I glowed, polished till I shone like a guardsman's toe-cap and sent to my mate's house. There we would sit on horse-hair chairs draped with antimacassars in the best room, which was only used on Messiah days or when someone died.

I can smell the musty scent of that room even now. I can see the twilight filtering through lace curtains that were only ever moved an inch to see who was passing by. We would gather in the room to sip elderberry wine – which was the nearest my mate's parents ever got to a rave-up. Then we would be off to the chapel to sit on spine-breaking benches while the local lads in the choir belted out the words with real vigour, without moving a strand of their concreted hair; and the visiting soloists, with quivering adam's apples and jellied bosoms, won a bonus point from the Almighty and a few quid in the back pocket as well.

Like all mining communities it was enclosed and self-sufficient. Visitors were welcome but likely to be regarded with friendly curiosity rather than real warmth. The cockney evacuees who came to our village were not treated as waifs but strangers from another planet. They could have been Martians for all we knew.

The first real-life American I ever saw was a soldier who was going out with one of the local girls. He looked like an extra from *Hollywood Canteen* or some such movie and I followed him and his girlfriend wherever they went with eyes stuck out like chapel hat-pegs. I was convinced he lived at The Rock with John Wayne.

It was a village where nothing was secret, where any private family crisis very soon became common knowledge. This meant, in the main, a caring community, but it could also be a cruel one.

I remember a girl, blonde and attractive, who became pregnant without first bothering to get married. I was standing at a bus-stop one day and she passed by, carrying her sin in front of her. 'She ought to have it sewn up,' said a woman in the queue, loud enough for the girl to hear. Although, at the time, I wasn't exactly sure of what she meant, I was in no doubt about the sentiment.

Yet this was also a village where you didn't need to lock your back door, where real tragedy – like sudden bereavement – was coddled and anaesthetised by genuine concern; where no child would ever be an orphan.

It was also a place of ritual where the horrid hours spent underground getting coal were countered with leisure activities that were seriously worked at. There was nothing dilettante about the allotment men, pigeon fanciers, cricketers, whippet breeders, part-time singers and snooker players.

Recreation was the antidote to a life-time working down the mine and therefore something to be taken seriously. You didn't play cricket for fun, nor grow parsnips only to eat. These activities were taken up to prove that you were the *best* cricketer in Cudworth or that you could grow the *biggest* parsnip. And if you didn't shape up that was all the more reason to work much harder at your hobby.

Boozing, too, was an antidote and a ritual. If I carry one lasting memory of life in a Yorkshire pit village it is of the moment before the pubs opened on Sunday lunch-time.

Ten minutes before noon the clients would congregate in little, silent groups a fair distance from the closed doors. With 30 seconds to opening time, and without anyone looking at a watch, they would move with unhurried tread towards the pub. As they arrived at the door it would open, as if by magic. If it didn't, it was the landlord who had got it wrong and never the lads. What is more, he would likely need a new door.

Having been around a bit since I left there I can't think of another place I would rather have grown up in. There are prettier places, no doubt, and healthier, too. But none where you felt that body-warmth, that sense of being an ordinary, vulnerable human both taking from and giving to those around you. That is not a nostalgic statement, rather a definition of my taproots.

'I was a runner.'

My Old Man

I was never told fairy tales as a child. Instead I heard of Larwood's action and Hobbs's perfection. Before I ever saw him play I knew Len Hutton intimately, and the first time I witnessed Stanley Matthews in the flesh I knew which way he was going even if the full-back didn't. The stories of these gods, and many, many more besides I heard at my father's knee.

He was a remarkable man with a marvellous facility to adorn an anecdote. It was he who invented the gate, complete with attendant, which was built in honour of a Barnsley winger who could run like the wind but didn't know how to stop. At the end of one of his runs down the wing the gate would be

'fear of being blinded by flying chips of concrete'

4

open and the winger would career through and out of the ground to finally come to a stop halfway across the car park. Or so Dad said.

It was he who told me of the full-back whose fearsome sliding tackles carried him into a wall surrounding the ground causing the spectators to start wearing goggles at home games for fear of being blinded by flying chips of concrete. Frank Barson, he assured me, once ran the entire length of the field bouncing the ball on his head, beat the opposing goalkeeper and then headed his final effort over the cross bar because he'd had a row with his manager before the game.

Moreover, the old man swore he managed to see Len Hutton's 364 at The Oval by convincing the gate attendant that he was dying of some incurable disease and his last wish was to see Len before he took leave of this earth. I never swallowed that one until once at a football match where the gates were closed I witnessed him convince a gateman that he was a journalist and I was his runner. I was seven at the time, and it was the very first occasion I watched a football match from a press box.

Apart from being a fairy story teller he was one of the best all-round sportsmen I have come across. He loved any game, and as soon as he took it up he played it well. I never saw him play football, but I have been told that he did a fair imitation of Wilf Copping. As a cricketer he was a quick bowler with an action copied from his great hero, Harold Larwood.

He had a marvellous agility and sure pair of hands near the bat, and as a batsman he was a genuine No. 11 who often didn't know whether he'd play left- or right-handed until he got to the crease. Not that it made much difference.

Of all games he loved cricket the most. He judged everything and everyone by the game. The only time I ever saw him lost for words was when someone confessed they neither knew nor cared about cricket. Then he would shake his head sadly baffled that a great part of his world – for cricket was surely that – could mean so little to any other sane human being. Once a friend and I took him to Headingley and sat him behind the bowler's arm and he never moved all day. We brought him pork pies and sandwiches and good Yorkshire beer, and he sat under his native sun watching Lillee bowl fast and he was the happiest man on our planet.

5

You always knew where my old man would be on any cricket ground: right behind the bowler's arm. Moreover, if ever you lost him, or he lost himself – as he often did being born without a sense of direction – you simply asked the whereabouts of the nearest cricket ground and there you would discover the old man sitting contentedly awaiting the arrival of his search party.

In his younger days his favourite holiday was a week at Scarbro' – which he reckoned had the best beach wicket in Britain – or Butlin's, not because he particularly cared for the idea of a holiday camp, but because of the sporting competitions. He used to enter the lot and normally came home with a couple of trophies for snooker or running or the mixed wheelbarrow race. He entered everything and anything and owed much of his success to his ability to talk an opponent to death. I once heard an irate tennis opponent say to him: 'Doesn't tha' ever shut thi' gob?'

'Only when other people are talking,' said my old man, with a disarming smile.

When he finished playing he took up coaching, first the local youngsters and latterly his three grandchildren. They, like me, are left-handed batsmen. Not because God made them so, but because the old man's theory was that not many players like bowling at left-handers. His other theory, based on a lifetime's experience, was that fast bowlers are crazy, so he determined to make at least one of my sons a slow bowler.

The consequence of this is that I once had the only eight-year-old googly bowler in the Western Hemisphere. At ten he added the top spinner to his repertoire and when he was twelve the old man's face was a picture as his protégé beat me with a googly and then had me plumb in front of the dustbin with one that hurried off the pitch and came straight through.

The old man's name was John William, and he hated John Willy. If anyone addressed him thus when he was playing in his prime, the red alert went up and the casualty ward at Barnsley Beckett Hospital could look forward to receiving visitors.

I have written a lot about him in my many years of writing about cricket, mainly in *The Sunday Times*; indeed the whole basic idea of any cricket article – a mixture of nostalgia and humour – was built on what I had heard at my father's knee.

He's been dead for a few cricket seasons now, but I still think about him because he was a special man and I was lucky to know him. He was a Yorkshireman, a miner, a humorist and a fast bowler. Not a bad combination.

I only hope they play cricket in heaven. If they don't he'll ask for a transfer.

'What's Bred in the Bone'

When I was born my paternal grandmother tried very hard to have me called Melbourne because MCC had just won a test match there. Fortunately my mother, a southerner of great common sense, would have none of it. Not so my father who, being a Yorkshireman and therefore cricket mad, was torn between Herbert (Sutcliffe), Percy (Holmes) or Hedley (Verity). Mother, fortunately, settled for Michael and would not budge. That was the only concession my old man made during the next twenty years which he devoted to producing a son who would one day play for Yorkshire.

At eleven I was playing in the team he captained, a child among men, a pimple among muscles. But I received no quarter because the old man would not have it that way. That I survived that period intact, considering the atrocious wickets we played on and the psychotic bowlers we faced, was due to my own fleet footedness and not as my father used to insist to the rumour that God protected prospective Yorkshire cricketers. He based this on the fact that He was born just outside Barnsley.

After every game came the post mortem, the old man dissecting every innings I played, advising, criticising, stuffing my young head with the game's folk lore. There was nothing selfish in this. He would have done the same for any kid my age because he couldn't stand the game being played badly. Only once did he use my tender years to his advantage. We were playing at a ground near Barnsley on a wicket which gave every impression of being prepared by a mechanical trench digger. We got our opponents out for about 40 and were in trouble at 24 for 7 when the old man joined me at the wicket. He came to me and said:

'Just keep your head down and leave the rest to me.'

He walked to the non-striker's end and immediately engaged in conversation with their fast bowler who had taken five wickets and put two of our players into the casualty ward.

As the fast bowler walked back to his mark the old man walked with him.

'Long run for an off spinner,' he said as they walked side by side.

'Wheer's tha' think tha's going?' said the fast bowler, stopping on his walk back.

'Wi' thee,' said the old man.

'Ay up umpire,' said the bowler. 'Can't tha' stop him?'

The umpire shook his head.

'Nowt in t'rules says he can't walk alongside thee lad,' said the umpire.

At the end of his walk back the bowler turned and began his run to the wicket and the old man kept pace with him stride for stride. Halfway to the wicket the bowler stopped.

'Ay up umpire can't tha' see what he's doing,' said the bowler to the umpire at square leg.

'Ay, he's running alongside thee lad but there's nowt to say he can't,' said the umpire.

The bowler shadowed everywhere by my old man completely lost his head and bowled three balls which nearly killed third slip. After the third he turned to my old man and addressed him in what I understood to be called 'pit language'. The old man listened for a while and then turned to the umpire and said:

'Did tha' hear that Charlie?'

'I did that Sammy,' said Charlie.

'Does tha' reckon it's fit language for a schoolboy to hear?'

'No,' said Charlie firmly.

'Then we're off and claiming maximum points,' said the old man and marched from the field, taking me with him.

As we walked off I pointed out that I had heard that kind of language and worse before so why had he taken umbrage?

'Tactics,' he said.

He proved his case by taking his action to the League Committee and being awarded maximum points for a game we hadn't a hope of winning.

Soon after I left his team to play for Barnsley in the Yorkshire League. But he followed, giving up playing to watch me. When I batted he would stand by the sightscreen semaphoring his displeasure onto the field by a series of anguished body contortions. His most spectacular demonstrations always occurred whenever I tried a late cut and missed. He believed firmly with Maurice Leyland that you never late cut before June and even then only if the moon had turned to green cheese. I once played this shot in a game at Barnsley and missed and looked toward the sightscreen where the old man was going through his paroxysm of displeasure. As I watched the stumper approached me.

'Are tha' watching what I'm watching?' he said.

I nodded.

'I reckon he's having a bloody fit,' said the stumper.

Whenever I got near a fifty he couldn't bear to watch and always spent ten minutes in the gent's toilet until the crowd noise informed him that I was either on 50 or out. I went to one fifty by hitting the ball into that very same toilet where it was fielded by my old man who came out holding the ball gingerly but looking like a man who has found a gold nugget.

Webb

When I was five years old, the old man bought me a cricket bat. The blade was creamy, the handle red, and it was the best bat I ever possessed.

I picked it up for the first time and stood in the approved position, left shoulder pointing down the wicket, left toe cocked in honour of George Roberts, the local big hitter, who at the time I considered the best batsman in the world. My old man patiently took the bat from me, turned me so my right shoulder pointed down the wicket and nodded in satisfaction. Thus, a left-handed bat was created against nature's whims.

I didn't question the move at the time, but later the old man explained everything. 'No bowler likes left-handers lad. Remember that and think on that you've got a head start.' As a bowler himself he reckoned he knew what he was talking about. He hated bowling at 'caggy handers'.

When he finished bowling and became captain of our second team he worked on the simple philosophy that the more left-handed batsmen he could discover or invent the better our chances of victory. He proved his point by winning the championship with a team which included nine left-handed bats, four natural, five manufactured. He took great delight in the freakish nature of his team and loved observing the mounting incredulity of his opponents as left-handed bat followed left-handed bat to the wicket. After the first half dozen, the opposing captain would often turn to the old man, lurking on the boundary edge, and say, 'Ayup skipper. 'Ow many more bloody caggy 'anders siree?'

Whenever I think about that team I always begin wondering about the number of people who affect our outlook and attitudes on sport. I am cricket mad because I caught the complaint from my old man, but even that condition might have been cured had it not been for someone else. He was the sports master at the local grammar school, a large craggy man who had been good enough to play both football and cricket at professional level.

The first time I came across him he was bowling at the nets at

11

we youngsters who were hoping to make the under-14 team. His first ball to me was a little short of a length and being young and full of madness I went for a hook and missed by a mile. It didn't seem very important to me and I was therefore a little taken aback on returning the ball to see the master, hands on hips, staring at the sky. He remained like that for some time, lips moving silently, and then he looked at me.

'What was that?' he asked.

'A hook sir,' I said. 'Hook?' he said shaking his head. 'A hook? At your age you shouldn't even know what it means.'

It was the best possible introduction to the man who for the next four years was to coach me in the game. He taught in the great Yorkshire tradition, concentrating solely on backward and forward defensive play. Any strokes we played that required the bat moving from the perpendicular were better done when he wasn't looking. I once played a late cut for four in a school game when I thought he was in bed with 'flu and as my eyes proudly followed the ball to the boundary, I saw him standing there sadly shaking his head at the horror of it all.

I once heard him admonish another master whom he caught demonstrating the square cut to a young player: 'Be it on your own head.'

For all he was a puritan about cricket he was a marvellous coach. He turned out a succession of young cricketers who were so well versed in the rudiments of the game that they found the transition from schoolboy cricket to the leagues fairly painless.

His one blind spot was a total inability to appreciate the odd exceptional talent that came his way. Everyone had to conform to his basic principles no matter how rich their natural gifts. At the time I was at school we had in our team a batsman called Hector of remarkable ability.

Hector, who was shaped like a junior Colin Milburn, had no time for acquiring defensive techniques. He approached each ball as if it was the last he would ever receive on this earth, and that being the case, he was going to try to split it in two. For a schoolboy he was an exceptional striker of the ball, blessed with a powerful physique, a quick eye and a sure sense of timing. He played some fine innings for the school teams, but no matter how brilliantly he played, he never pleased the sports master.

'Defence, Hector lad, defence,' the sports master would say, and Hector would put one foot down the track and blast the ball straight for six and the sports master would look sorrowful. The high point of their relationship occurred in a masters versus boys game in which the sports master opened the bowling and Hector opened the batting. He played one of his best innings that day, thrashing the bowling, particularly the sport master's, without mercy.

The master kept the ball up as he always taught us to do, and Hector kept thumping away. He had scored about 86 in 30 minutes when he hit over one of the sports master's deliveries and was bowled. As he walked towards the pavilion the sports master said triumphantly: 'I warned you Hector lad, that's what fancy play gets you.'

He was the only man on the field, or off it, who remained convinced that Hector had failed. It would have pleased him more if Hector had observed the rules that bound us lesser players and carried his bat for a dour thirty.

But for all that, he was a good man who taught a lot of boys a proper respect for the most difficult and beautiful of games.

When I saw him last, he looked old and ill and said he had retired as a sports master. He told me he watched the school team occasionally but had invariably been disappointed by what he saw. 'Too much flashing about, not enough straight bat,' he said.

He stood up to demonstrate his point. 'Cricket is about this . . .' He played forward with an imaginary bat. 'And this . . .' He played back. 'And not this . . .' And he executed what I can only describe as a derogatory late cut.

His name was Webb Swift and I heard recently that he had died. The chances are you've never heard of him. He wasn't a famous man, just important to a lot of people like me who learnt to love cricket at his knee, and whenever I think about people who have affected my life, I remember him.

Demolition Expert

My father was a man who treasured his possessions. In his sporting days his cricket boots were blancoed to perfection, his whites were whiter than, and his bat, which must have been used by W. G. Grace, was cleaned and oiled like a new-born child. Similarly his football boots were dubbined until they were as supple as kid and then polished until they gleamed like shiny black dancing-pumps.

When he bought a car, an ancient and world-weary Triumph, he didn't leave it in the street to spend its final years in the gutter, he built a garage for it. Considering the state of the vehicle this was something like building a solarium for a corpse. Being blessed with considerable ingenuity but no money, father decided to construct his own garage. The fact that he had built nothing more complicated than a rabbit hutch in no way deterred him.

After assembling a pile of railway sleepers, pit props and orange boxes he nailed the lot together with six-inch nails and painted the doors green. It would never have won an award for elegance and looked so ramshackle that it afforded much hilarity among the neighbours, but it was, in fact, an overcoat for my father's proudest possession, and that is all he cared about.

What he didn't realise was that I had different uses for his garage and it was to play an important part in my sporting education. In those days when street lamps were our wickets and two coats our goal-posts the garage became Lord's and Wembley all rolled into one. We chalked three stumps on the doors that were also our goals, and on alternate days, until the soccer season faded and cricket took over, the garage became the focal point of all our fantasies.

It was here that Barnsley won the cup final three years running from 1947 to 1950 and on each occasion I scored the winning goal in extra time. It was here that Len Hutton's record Test score of 364 was surpassed by another young Yorkshireman called Tiger Parkinson who smote Lindwall,

Miller *et al.* all over the county before retiring with a broken bat for an undefeated 527.

The same player was well on the way to surpassing even that mammoth score when there occurred one of those traumatic incidents that so affect the life of the budding sportsman. Swinging hard to leg to hook yet another six I pivoted around, bat flailing, and hit the corner of the garage, whereupon the whole structure sighed, creaked, and fell apart like a pack of cards. My father's anger was increased by the knowledge that his garage had been demolished by the kind of stroke he disapproved of and I had the definite impression that had it been collapsed in the execution of a proper defensive stroke nothing would have been said about it.

We built our next garage out of bricks, knocking down a couple of old air-raid shelters to get the materials, and my penance for a rash stroke was to sit at home when I ought to have been practising my shots, chopping away mortar from bricks that had been built to withstand bombs. The new gar-

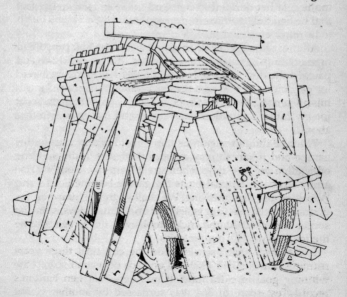

'the whole structure sighed, creaked, and fell apart like a pack of cards'

age, again constructed by my father without recourse to any professional advice, was so lop-sided that it made the Leaning Tower of Pisa look like Centre Point.

Local brickies would make detours to marvel at the unique skill of someone who could build sloping garages. I was present when one of them, goggling in awe, was approached by my old man. 'What's tha' reckon?' asked father. The brickie thought for a bit and then said: 'Ah reckon tha' ought to stick to fast bowling.' No matter what the building profession thought about our garage my old man was determined that it should not be used for purposes other than for which it was constructed. This meant an end to our practice facilities.

To soften our disappointment the old man persuaded the committee at the cricket club to build a concrete practice strip. The committee agreed on condition that father took no part in its construction and decided that while they were at it they would build a toilet next to the pavilion, several lady members having objected to the sight of grown men standing up against the hedge surrounding the ground trying to look nonchalant and pretending they were bird nesting.

In our tiny world such a plan constituted an event, and therefore it was decided the new pitch and the toilet should be opened by the chairman of the council. A major problem was finding a net to enclose the practice pitch, and this we achieved by persuading the soccer club to part with one of their goal nets. The fact that a net designed for stopping footballs is not likely to be ideal when used for cricket never occurred to us – until it was too late.

The day before the grand opening, with a full-scale rehearsal for the civic ceremony of our toilet going on nearby, we decided to try out the pitch. I had the honour of taking first strike and, wanting to give it a proper baptism, decided that whatever was bowled at me I was going to give it a go. Unfortunately the first ball was a long hop outside the leg stump and foolishly I played the shot that had already demolished a garage.

I was fully aware of what I was doing, reasoning that the net would stop the ball. It didn't. The fact is a cricket ball will pass through a football net like a draught through an open window. The ball whistled through the net as if it wasn't there, broke the window of the new toilet with a noise like a gunshot and shattered the shiny new flush toilet tank into a thousand pieces.

In the moment I stood transfixed with horror at what I had done, the toilet door burst open and there stood our secretary, trousers round his ankles, covered in fragments of toilet-ware, holding the lavatory chain in his hand. It later transpired that he was giving the toilet a dress rehearsal and had just pulled the chain when the whole thing exploded. His immediate horror at the thought he might have pulled too hard, or alternatively been the victim of some monstrous practical joke was in no way alleviated when he learned the truth.

The civic opening was postponed, and until we'd found the money for a new lav we spent several weeks in the hedges

'there stood our secretary, trousers round his ankles . . .'

pretending we were bird nesting. The old man had a theory, that had they let him build the toilet it would have leaned so much that the ball would have missed. That's as may be. All I know is that it was ages before I ever attempted the hook shot.

Many years later, playing with another club, I was batting against a bowler who was trundling up what could most generously be described as rubbish. He bowled me a long hop outside the leg stump and I couldn't resist it. I gave it an almighty whack only to be caught one-handed and brilliantly by a youth standing on the boundary. Had he not been there it would have been a six. Later in the bar the bowler said to me, 'I found thi' weakness.' That was pretty funny. What he didn't know was that with my kind of luck, if the fielder hadn't caught the ball I would most likely have knocked the pavilion down.

Unsung Heroes

When I was very young and dreaming of being Len Hutton – that was in the days when England had a cricket team – a cricket pitch was any strip of land approximately twenty-two yards long. The first floodlit cricket match ever played was between my Invitation XI and Gonk Reynolds' team under a street lamp in a Yorkshire mining village near on thirty years ago. Wisden does not record the fact, but at that time we didn't know who he was either.

In those earliest formative years the art of batmanship was a simple matter of protecting your person rather than defending the wicket. The present crop of England cricketers who play Lillee and Thomson from square leg remind me irresistibly of my old team who knew that to follow the classic dictum of getting the nose over the ball simply meant a two-ounce missile up the left nostril.

Our best pitch was a strip of brown earth near the top boozer. We ironed out the lumps by jumping on them and flattened it into submission with the back of a coal shovel. In the end it resembled the colour and texture of treacle toffee, but at least it drew the teeth of our budding fast bowlers who either learned to pitch it up or, alternatively, joined the card school which rivalled drinking as the favourite pastime in our village.

Equipment was a problem. We had two bats, one made from a railway sleeper which must have weighed ten pounds and was like batting with a sledgehammer, and the other an aged Patsy Hendren autograph bat which had half the blade sawn off so that we kids could handle it. Balls were 'corkies', which had the killing power of cannon balls, sometimes supplemented by wooden balls which we nicked from the coconut shies of the travelling fairs.

In order to raise funds for new equipment we used to lie in wait for the punters from the top boozer. At chucking-out time you could always reckon on a crowd of them lurching across our pitch.

We used to say: 'Bet tha' can't bowl me out mister.' The punter, awash in Barnsley Bitter, would always rise to the challenge. 'How much kid?' he'd say. 'I'll bet thee a tanner tha' can't get me out in twenty balls,' we'd say.

They used to take their coats off, measure out their runs and come charging in like fighting bulls. What happened as they approached the delivery crease always depended on how much they had supped. Some expired in the final stride, some got lost on the way, often ending up facing the establishment they had just left and bowling at the tap-room door.

The few that managed to propel the ball in the general direction of the snotty-nosed kid with the railway sleeper in his hand were soon discouraged by the pitch which suffocated the ball's venom and smothered the bowler's ambition. They'd pay up and go home muttering. On a good day we'd end up with a couple of bob apiece. They didn't know it then but they were, in fact, cricket's first sponsors. Again Wisden didn't record the fact, but, then again, I'll bet he didn't spend much time in the snug at our local boozer.

As far as wickets were concerned, things didn't get better when I joined my first club. The wicket was what could be politely termed 'sporting'.

It wasn't the fault of the groundsman, a lovely crotchety old soul called Cheyney. He tried hard, but there was too much wrong with the square ever to get it right.

Cheyney was a great believer in using animal droppings as fertilizer, and he always used to carry a bucket with him whenever he went about the village in case some horse along the way might oblige him with a dollop of dressing for his pitch. We had the dubious distinction of not only having one of the worst pitches in the world, but also the smelliest. At the same time you could argue that we had the cleanest streets in Britain because Cheyney's pursuit of horse droppings was tireless and meticulous.

He was once invited along to the local evening class to give a lecture on the art of being a groundsman. Being a man of few words, he didn't waste any. 'The secret of making grass grow is 'oss muck,' he said, and sat down.

The audience who expected a somewhat lengthier dissertation stirred uncomfortably. The chairman asked nervously: 'Surely there must be something else?' Cheyney shook his head: 'Nowt but more 'oss muck,' he replied.

Some time later, after old Cheyney was dead and buried, they built a super new sports stadium on the site of his wicket. They dedicated it to Dorothy Hyman, who was born in the village. I opened it amid much splendour and civic pomp, but nobody mentioned that it was built on a ton of Cheyney's horse manure.

It wasn't until I went to the local grammar school that I discovered the joy of batting on a proper wicket. The pitch was carved from a hillside high above Barnsley. It was an unlikely setting for a treasure, but there is no doubt in my mind that the wicket I played on for the next five seasons was the best batting track I have ever encountered. It was fast and true and in good weather possessed that lovely sheen which meant runs for anyone who could play straight and an afternoon of purgatory for any bowler who strayed from all but the strictest line and length.

About that time I had given up being Len Hutton in order to emulate my great hero, Keith Miller, but I quickly gave up all ambitions of being an all-rounder after my first bowl on that wicket. I went back to Len. Stouter hearts than mine tried to hammer some life out of it, but none succeeded. These bowlers were not only discouraged by the absolute perfection of the strip, but also by the attitude of the groundsman, John Matthewman.

He was a taciturn man, only moved to displays of emotion when fast bowlers with large feet ploughed up his precious turf. Then he would spend the game pacing the boundary muttering about the vandals who were trampling on his work of art. We once played against a team with a fast bowler who dragged his back foot alarmingly. Moreover, he possessed a pair of boots reinforced with steel plates which gave them the appearance of a pair of ironclads and did to our pitch what the invading Goths did to ancient Rome.

At the end of our innings the groundsman was beside himself with rage. He invited the offending bowler to inspect the damage he had caused. Together they stared at the scarred turf.

'Just look what tha's done,' said John, in sorrow and anger.

'Well, it's mi drag tha' sees,' said the bowler.

'Drag?' said John.

'Tha' sees I drag mi toe when I'm bowling,' the bowler explained.

'Whoever bowled on his sodding toes. Whoever heard of such a thing,' said John. 'Anyway what's them?' he asked, indicating the player's boots.

'Reinforced toe-caps,' the bowler said.

'Reinforced toe-caps. I've nivver heard of anything so daft. They look like bloody pit boots. Bowling on his toes with pit boots on. A bloody ballet dancer wearing pit boots. Whoever heard of such a thing,' said John, by now on his knees trying to repair the damage.

If the idiosyncrasies of fast bowlers were a complete and

'the groundsman was beside himself with rage'

22

utter mystery to him there wasn't a single thing he didn't know about the preparation of a cricket pitch. Before we were allowed to set foot on one of his masterpieces he inspected it inch by inch armed with a cut-throat razor, trimming a blade of grass that dared to be a millimetre out of uniform length, slitting the throat of any weed that had the audacity to believe it might flourish while he was around. When he had finished he would give us the nod.

'What's it like?' we'd say, as part of the ritual.

'If tha' can play cricket tha'll get runs,' was what he'd always reply. And he was as good as his word.

When I left that school I moved down the hill to Barnsley Cricket Club and, shortly after, John Matthewman came down, too. Ask any knowledgeable cricketer to name the best batting tracks in Yorkshire and John Matthewman's Barnsley wicket is sure to be mentioned.

Whenever I think back on the game I love most of all I remember that slab of earth in a Yorkshire pit village where I first played the game and then of John Matthewman's two masterpieces where I learned to play the game properly. I calculate the difference and in doing so assess what I and hundreds of other players owe to John Matthewman and people like him.

I thought of him a lot when I heard he had died. A local death not warranting a mention in the national press. A groundsman dies, a man whose simple job it was to shape earth, grass, wind, rain and sun into a cricket pitch. On the face of it that is all there is to it. Yet I know he was an artist, and so do many others who were acquainted with his work. Often he achieved perfection, and how many of us will go to the grave able to say that one, ultimately fulfilling, thing?

The Debut

The first time you play cricket with the big boys is like your first love affair or the first taste of shandy on a sweaty day – something you will remember for the rest of your life. I go back thirty years to the time I walked onto a cricket field with what my father always called 'proper' cricketers, which is to say men who didn't muck about on the field of play.

I can remember it vividly to this day: I can recall the dressing room smell of sweat and liniment and linseed oil, I can see the clothes hanging on the nails that served as pegs, and I remember my heroes one by one. The local hitter was Mr Roberts. He had a false leg and I often wondered what it looked like. Well, I found out that day they played me in the first team. The other hitter, Mr Stewardson, had a bat bound in brown leather and tacked up the back of the blade. He used to clout the ball immense distances and attributed his success to the bat which he had used for ten years or more. When asked about the binding he would look around him in conspiratorial fashion to make sure that no one else was listening and whisper 'Kangaroo skin, tha' sees.' The questioner would nod wisely as if it was common knowledge that kangaroo skin on a cricket bat would make the ball leap from its surface.

Mr Berry was our spin bowler and probably the most gifted player in the side. He bowled leg breaks at about Underwood's pace and, when the mood took him, was unplayable. What I always wanted to know about him, however, was how he kept his sleeves up when he bowled. As someone who always contrived to look like an unmade bed after six overs in the field, I was envious of Mr Berry's ability to play through the longest and hottest day with not a ruffle in his outline and not a shirtsleeve out of place. I watched him dress but never did find out the secret and dared not ask him in case he thought I was daft, or a wrong 'un, or both.

The quick bowlers were my old man and Mr Baker who had the longest run in local cricket. It was nothing for him to start his run from behind the sightscreen and on one ground, where

24

there was a gate behind the bowler's arm, he actually started outside the field, bursting onto the scene like a runaway horse. Actually he had a gliding, smooth approach to the wicket and was a good-looking man with a handsome profile, and a liking for curved pipes and gentle conversation. By comparison his opening partner, my old man, was a volatile and explosive cricketer who expected, nay demanded, a wicket with every ball he bowled and woe betide any fielder with trembling fingers who stood between him and his ambition.

Our wicket-keeper was called Minty and he was a huge man with a bald head and a look of Telly Savalas. He wore the biggest protector I have ever seen, and he needed to because he stood up to every bowler no matter what the pace or the state of the wicket. His simple theory of wicket-keeping was that the job involved stopping a cricket ball with any part of the anatomy available which accounted for his extra large protector and the bruises that covered him from head to foot after every game.

Those were a few of the people I shared the pavilion with

'Sharing the pavilion with Mr Berry and Minty'

some thirty years ago on a hot August day when I made my debut with the local side. I was eleven or twelve at the time, a tin-tack in amongst the six-inch nails. I knew I wouldn't get a bat or a bowl and that I mustn't make a mistake in the field or else I'd get murdered by the old man when I got home. On paper it seems a daunting prospect, but to me at that time it was the highlight of my life.

Two things happened in the game to convince me that I was right to want to be Len Hutton. The first was that someone swore on the field, using a word that in those days you would never use in front of eleven-year-old innocents. I looked quickly at my old man to see his reaction, but he just looked at me and winked, and I knew at that moment that I had been accepted into the brotherhood of cricketers and was not an imposter.

But the most marvellous moment came when I made a catch. It was a straightforward effort but I held it, and I knew they'd have to put my name on the score book and there would be proof of my existence. Moreover there was a chance I might get a mention in the local paper, but it didn't happen. Mind you I made up for the lack of publicity much later when I was working as a reporter on the local paper and also playing cricket every weekend. Then I wrote my own reports and became the best publicised player in South Yorkshire. Headlines like: 'PARKINSON AGAIN' or 'ANOTHER PARKINSON TRIUMPH' were a commonplace in our local paper and even in the lean times the readers were guaranteed a 'PARKINSON FAILS' headline every now and again just to keep the name fresh in their minds.

All these memories came drifting deliciously back when my nine-year-old was asked to make his debut with the local club. The other two were already veterans, having been blooded young, but the little one I was holding back on the advice of his Uncle Geoff who had been working on the forward defensive stroke and Uncle Illy who had been showing how to get side-on in the delivery stride.

We knew of his selection the day before the game but didn't dare break the news to him until the next morning in order for him to sleep in untroubled peace. Otherwise the only way we could have persuaded him to have closed his eyes was by giving him a bottle of sleeping tablets and half a bottle of scotch. He took the field looking like an advert for soap powder and a quick check around the field revealed that the only other participants smaller than him were the stumps.

He was hidden by the captain (who happened to be his elder brother acting on my instructions) in all the places where you don't expect a cricket ball to go whereupon, inevitably, the opposition hit the ball to all those places where you don't expect a cricket ball to go. Still, he fielded well and earned my particular admiration for sensibly going the other way to a fierce top edge that would have given Derek Randall trouble.

But his big moment came when he had to come in at number two to play out the last over. The opposition kindly looped gentle spin at him whereby he nearly decapitated short leg with a brusque pull off the middle of his bat. He came off flushed as a drunken sailor with three not out, and I immediately informed Alec of his availability. That was on a Monday. On Friday before he went to school I saw him looking at the sports pages in the local paper, and I knew what he was seeking. He looked in vain. I couldn't tell him what I knew, that you don't need a yellowed cutting to remind you of your first game with proper cricketers. It is burned in your mind forever.

Let Battle Commence

My cricket seasons always began at Bramall Lane, Sheffield, in Stygian gloom, with the clouds so low they sat on the football stands and we seemed to be playing in a darkened corridor. Those dreamers who see cricket as a sunlit game with creamy figures flitting hither and thither throwing graceful shadows should try Bramall Lane in April.

Those who are prepared to face the truth could not wish a better introduction. First there was the wicket itself. The rumour is that they don't cut the grass in Sheffield, just roll it flat. And certainly one could bring forward as evidence many cricketers, all sober men with 20/20 vision, who would swear to having seen the grass rising in front of them in the opening overs of a game. Ordinarily it wouldn't matter too much, but it made a deal of difference when we played at Bramall Lane because it meant we had to face George Pope.

Given a combination of the new ball, a succulent wicket and the clouds low and heavy, George Pope, on an April afternoon in Sheffield, was capable of bowling out any side in the world. He was, of course, one of the most devastating seam bowlers ever reared in Derbyshire, which is another way of saying he was one of the best in the world. To face him in the first few minutes of a brand new season was an experience comparable to being beaten with a soft cosh on the day you were born. It left you with no illusions about the future.

I played against him for four seasons in these circumstances, which explains why I love cricket as a cynical bitch of a mistress instead of the crinolined lady most people take her for.

It wasn't just George Pope's absolute mastery of the art of bowling that taught you the whole lesson, it was also his complete understanding of cricket psychology. Once, after being clobbered for a magnificent six by a brave and unrazored youth Pope remarked with a benign smile 'They go a lot further when you middle them sonny.' He then brought up an extra short leg and bowled him next ball. His manipulation of umpires is worth a chapter in any book on psychology.

It would start as soon as they met in the middle.

'Good day, Mr Umpire,' said George.

'Good day, George,' said the umpire, slightly flattered at being singled out by the great man.

'Not very pleasant for the time of year,' said George.

'Terrible.'

'I always say that you chaps earn your money turning out in stuff like this. And how's the lumbago?' asked George.

'Playing up a bit thank you,' said the umpire, surprised he should know about it.

'And how are your roses this year?' George asked.

'Look very promising,' said the umpire, by now beside himself with joy that this man should be so concerned with both his passions and his problems.

From then on the batsman was doomed.

The first time Pope hit the pads, usually with a massive inswinger that would have finished life at square leg, he would turn to the umpire, smile and say:

'Not quite, I think, not quite.'

The next time there would be a strangled appeal from George and an immediate apology. 'Sorry Mr Umpire, again not quite. You were quite right to ignore me.'

The umpire was still congratulating himself on his exquisite judgment when George would strike again, but this time with an appeal you could hear in Manchester.

And this time the umpire, who by now was so fond of George he was entertaining thoughts of adopting him, would put his finger up. It never failed. The only consolation to the batsman was that it really didn't make much difference because had Pope not chosen to get you LBW in that particular way, he could have bowled you any time he wanted to.

The fact that George Pope is now a county umpire is the classic instance of a poacher turning gamekeeper.

Our encounter with Pope at Bramall Lane always developed into verbal battles of rare quality between him and Ellis Robinson. Robinson was our professional. He had played cricket for Yorkshire and Somerset and was an off-spinner of imagination and real skill.

The classic Robinson-Pope meeting came the Saturday after Blackpool had beaten Bolton in the cup final. Bramall Lane that day was a seductive, lush strip of turf made to measure for

George Pope and his art and he didn't conceal his delight when Sheffield won the toss and sent us in.

'Fancy thi' chances then Ellis,' he yelled through our dressing room door.

'I'll gi' thee some stick this afternoon Popey. Ah can bat thee wi' mi' cap neb,' replied Ellis.

But it was Popey's day and not all of Robinson's optimism or skill could prevent it.

Ellis came in about fourth wicket down with few runs on the board and Popey swinging them like boomerangs.

He walked slowly to the crease, taking his time, adjusting his eyes to the light, sizing things up. He took guard, touched his Yorkshire cap and looked hard at Popey standing in the slips. 'Na' then Ellis, are tha' going to get any chalks?'

'Reckon on 50 George.'

'I'm doing a bit today tha' knows Ellis.'

'Tha' nivver could bowl.'

Robinson settles into his stance. The bowler begins his run. Tap-tap, bat on crease. An outswinger, Robinson forward. Misses. Stumper takes it.

Pope (looking up at heaven): 'Jesus Christ Ellis. Tha' allus wor lucky.'

'Lucky be buggered. I let the bloody thing past.'

'Nivver. Nivver. Tha' nivver saw it.'

And so on, until Pope was bowling which prevented him from talking, but not Robinson who now conversed with which ever fielder happened to be the nearest.

'Fancy thi' chances does tha' lad? Be careful. I wouldn't like to face meself on this track today. Not today I wouldn't. Oh no.'

Pope approaching the crease. Loose, almost affable action. Not so quick as he used to be but twice as crafty. Right to the far edge of the bowling crease. Immaculate length. Ball pushed diagonally at the leg stump. A lot of cut on it. Hits pitch and snaps back, beats the bat and catches Robinson high on the front pad as he pushes forward Pope whips around, glowers at the umpire for a second and then lets one go which rattles the pavilion windows.

'Owzat?'

'Not out,' says the umpire.

'And I should bloody well think not,' shouts Robinson from

the other end of the pitch, 'it wouldn't have hit a set of stumps six feet high.'

Pope glares at him down the track. Robinson glares back. There seems to be no one else in the whole of Bramall Lane except these two glaring and snarling at one another.

Pope turns on his heel and walks back to his mark. As he passes the umpire who is still trembling from the blast of the appeal, he says, in a soft, polite voice, 'A little high perhaps Mr Umpire?'

The umpire nods.

'Perhaps so,' says George, all smooth and buttery, 'but I thought I would enquire, you know.'

And so it went on. There was no holding Pope that day. Everything was right for him: the grass, green and damp and gripping the seam like a lover, making the ball change direction as if it had a mind of its own.

We were bowled out for under 50 and Pope took eight wickets for less than 20 runs. Our only reassurance was that he would have taken wickets against any team in the world on that track and in those conditions.

We were in with a chance with Robinson angry and a couple of useful seamers. But it rained during the interval and when play recommenced the wicket was wet and useless and Sheffield easily knocked off the runs. It was no good talking to Robinson as we changed for home. He kept muttering to himself, 'Bloody weather. I'd have shown Popey. Nivver could bowl. I'd have caused some panic.'

So we went into the bar to drown our sorrows and went home silently, in our special bus through the rain-misty, slimy streets of Sheffield with only a stop for a fish and six and a bag of scraps before we reached Barnsley.

We went to our own club bar where we told the second team just how much Popey had been bending them – exaggerating like anglers – until Saturday night slid away into Sunday morning when we woke up stiff as sergeant majors, certain now that the season had started. And glad.

Doing it for Money

The basic difference between the Southern and Northern cricketer is that one does it for money and the other for free. The fact that the Northern club cricketer is more serious about his game is partly due to breeding but more to do with the fact that a good performance with bat or ball will gain him a collection. This system of passing the hat round for someone who had made fifty or taken five wickets is in many ways the cornerstone of North Country cricket. It gives it a unique flavour, it turns Saturday afternoon sportsmen into hard-eyed professionals. There are Northern cricketers renowned as 'collection players'. These are the men who can guarantee that their Saturday evening booze-up will be paid for by the spectators. The best one I ever played with devoted his entire life to a study of the science of collection cricket. His comments about the weather were all to do with money.

'Good collection weather' he would say as the sun blazed down on the cricket field. After changing into his whites he would often go down to the turnstile to welcome the paying customers, rubbing his hands in the most obsequious manner, behaving like a head waiter. The simile is accurate because like a head waiter he was touting for tips. When he came back to the pavilion we'd ask: 'What's the crowd like Charlie?' 'Ten pounds twelve and six worth,' he'd say. This was Charlie's estimate of what the first collection would yield. He was never more than sixpence wrong. The collection was the best barometer of public opinion ever invented. It told the player precisely how much or how little he had entertained the spectators. My maiden fifty in club cricket left me elated. I returned to the pavilion like a champion, drunk with my talents, eager to gain my reward. 'How much?' I asked the skipper who was always entrusted with the collection. He pointed to the table where lay the contents of the collection boxes. The crowd had assessed my innings as being worth fourteen and sevenpence halfpenny made up entirely in half-pennies, two brass buttons, one blue tiddlywink and a badge which said I was now a member of the Flash Gordon Fan Club.

It was my introduction to the most honest criticism a player can ever have. People could flatter you with false words but when they were asked to put their money where their mouth was they spoke the truth. The criticism of the collection system is that it rewards individuals in what is essentially a team game. That is what the purists say, but I've always thought that cricket is the most selfish of games and that the collection system doesn't corrupt anyone; it is simply an honest antidote to all that bilge about playing for the sake of the club, country and general well-being of the soul. Once you've won a collection the money is yours to do with as you like; the only time you are expected to relinquish your loot is during a benefit game. Then the rule is that all collections are donated to the beneficiary who will then leave ten quid or so behind the bar for the team to get drunk on.

Benefit games are the cricketer's gold watch, an expression of gratitude by club and spectators to a player who has sacrificed most important things, including his wife and his liver, for their enjoyment.

'like a head waiter he was touting for tips'

Sometimes, though, they can go very wrong indeed. And when a benefit game turns nasty the difference between that and a normally keen cricket match is the difference between a tap-room brawl with broken bottles and a pillow fight in the dormitory.

I still carry the scars from one of these games. It occurred in those dear tender days when my only problem was deciding whether I'd like to be Keith Miller or Neville Cardus. I was playing for a team in the North and we agreed to stage a benefit game for a batsman who was the idol of the county. We had in the team at the time a gnarled old professional who had once played for the county and was now forced to earn his pennies in the leagues. He was a talented cricketer, a good enough spin bowler to have gone through the Australians on one occasion. But he never quite made the top.

His benefit year with the county had coincided with the monsoon season and he'd been kicked out of the game shortly after with a lot of memories and no money. He nursed his disenchantment savagely but quietly, until he got drunk, which was often, or until he had an off day and bowled badly, and then his fielders were showered with a rich and most original flow of abuse.

In one game he was pummelled by a large and unorthodox batsman who reckoned nothing to our professional's reputation nor his subtle snares of flight and spin. He simply put his front foot forward and thumped the ball with a frightening noise to all parts of the ground. Not to be bested our pro simply moved the leg trap closer. 'Gerrin closer. He can't ruddy well bat,' he would say as they retrieved the ball from the tennis courts.

I was the centre of the leg trap and frighteningly close. The batsman eyed me and grinned, 'Tha' for t'morgue standing theer,' he said pleasantly. And he was nearly right. He swung at the next ball, I ducked covering all my important parts and was struck a horrifying crack on the knee cap. The ball shot off my knee (I thought it had gone clean through it) to the boundary.

I lay there crippled wondering if I were alive or not when I saw our pro glowering down at me. 'What's matter, lightning?' he said. I muttered something about my knee and a doctor whereupon he said, bitterly, 'Tha' doesn't want medical treatment, tha' wants stuffin'.' It wasn't that he particularly disliked me. He treated everyone he played with or against with the same detached hostility.

Anyway he didn't want to play in this benefit game because he said he did not like the beneficiary. He was probably jealous because his benefit was a disaster and the man whose game he was asked to play in had already made a fortune out of cricket. But he was made to play. The captain and the committee insisted, which, as it turned out, was the worst decision they ever made.

The day of the game was perfect, the crowd large and ready to spend and the beneficiary arrived looking prosperous and happy. This joyful combination simply made our pro spend longer than usual in the bar before the game 'lubricating the arm', as he put it. By the time we took the field he was muttering gently to himself. Later someone said he was saying 'I'll fix 'im' over and over to himself, but that might be a case of inventing the quote after the event.

All went well for a while. The runs came briskly, our pro allowed himself to be thumped without recourse to violence on his colleagues and everyone was thinking what a pleasant occasion it was. Then came the moment the crowd had waited for. One of the openers was bowled by our pro and out came the beneficiary.

The crowd rose to him and cheered as he walked to the wicket. He looked around at them smiling and no doubt adding up how much a fifty would be worth. He arrived at the wicket and settled in to take first ball. Now the golden rule of benefit games is that the beneficiary is given an easy first ball to get him off the mark and feeling happy. The great batsman waited for the gift to be granted. But our pro ran up and bowled him the best off-break it has ever been anyone's misfortune to face. It pitched off stump to a good length, bit, spun sharply, turned inside the bat and flattened the leg stump. It would have bowled anyone in the world.

For a moment there was absolute, unbelieving silence on the ground. The batsmen looked poleaxed, our captain started going purple, the fielders hung their heads in embarrassment. The only person on the ground who looked pleased was our pro. He was standing by the umpire giggling gently to himself. There looked to be no solution. The great man had to go, bowled first ball in his benefit game. Fully 30 seconds had elapsed before the umpire at square leg came up with the answer. As the great batsman turned to walk away he shouted: 'No ball.'

Our pro stopped giggling and gaped in disbelief. Our captain knocked the leg stump back in, patted the great batsman on the back, and relegated our pro to the outfield where he spent the rest of the afternoon sulking. The great batsman, recovered now from the shock, went on to make fifty and the incident was forgotten until the tea interval when our skipper bawled out the pro for his misbehaviour.

But the pro's great moment was yet to come. After the game we gathered in the bar for the ritual of counting the money. There it was on the table, mountains of silver and copper. The Chairman announced that about £300 had been collected. This pleased us because form demanded that he leave at least £20 behind the bar so that the rest of us could get drunk at his expense. We had all worked up a splendid thirst when the great batsman arrived to collect his loot. He walked into the bar, scooped all the money into a small potato sack, shook hands with the chairman of the committee and walked out. No beer money, not even a thank you. We sat there hurt and angry by his ingratitude. For a long time nobody said a word and then the skipper turned to our pro and said 'Did 'tha' mean to bowl him first ball?'

'I did that,' said the pro.

'It wor a good un,' said our skipper nodding his head.

'Good enough,' said our pro.

'Come to think of it, it were just about the best ball I've ever seen,' said the skipper. And we all nodded wisely and settled into an evening of yarning and drinking, at our own expense. Later, after playing club cricket in the South I returned North and saw our professional. He asked me what kind of season I'd had and I told him I'd done quite well and made a few fifties. 'You'll be in the money then lad,' he said. I told him that they didn't have collections in the South. He stared at me in disbelief. 'No collections?' he said. I shook my head. 'Then the game's not worth playing is it?' he said. I agreed and I think I still do. I know that the pleasure of cricket is supposedly stored in the soul, but how much more pleasant if a little bit is also stashed in the bank.

The Next Man in is Walter Mitty

The nice thing about sport is that it brings out the Walter Mitty in all of us. From time to time I have opened for England with Boycott and rattled up a double century before lunch, beaten Jean Claude Killy with ridiculous ease in the Winter Olympics and regularly ridden a 100 to 1 outsider to spectacular victory in the Derby. This last one is my favourite fantasy because according to my dreams both the horse and the key to my heart are owned by a titled lady of great beauty and after my win we drink champagne and nibble goodies in her penthouse suite and she whispers softly to me: 'How do you do it Parky?' And I with becoming nonchalance reply: 'Really my lady it was nothing.'

Such dreams are beautiful and harmless. They only turn nasty when you try and make them come true. For instance even though I am confident that I could win Wimbledon any time I want I would never actually join the competition and take my chance against Borg and the like. I would rather sit at home in front of my television set nursing my superiority. Not all sports fantasists are as sensible. For instance a 55 year old American, Mr Homer Shoop, carried all his fantasies into real life when he partnered Gardner Mulloy in the veteran men's doubles at Wimbledon. There he stood on the number five court, partnered by a man who had once been tennis champion of America, ready to prove to all the world that Homer Shoop was a name to rank with the immortals of tennis.

Sadly and predictably, Mr Shoop had his dream shattered. The game, by his own admission, was 'ridiculous'. He and his partner lost 6–1, 6–4, the crowd laughed at them and Gardner Mulloy described what happened as a 'real pantomime' and a 'humiliation'. The unfortunate Homer Shoop did his best to restore his tattered dignity, by explaining, 'I had bad 'flu, a very bad left knee and a weak right wrist.'

Homer Shoop was not the first sportsman to fall foul of his dreams. I once played cricket with a young man who dreamed of being the Reverend David Sheppard. The fact that his real name was Horace, that he lived in the South Yorkshire coalfield, and that his Dad was regularly in the pawnshop with the old woman's wedding ring only increased his desire to become a gentleman cricketer of impeccable breeding. Nor was he deterred by the fact that he was a very ordinary cricketer trying to emulate one of the best batsmen in the world. He studied Sheppard in action for hours and practised in front of a mirror until he had managed an exact copy of that great batsman's stance at the wicket. He even copied Sheppard's hairstyle and mode of dress but failed at that too. When the rest of us were resplendent in slim jims, winklepickers, tight pants and crew cuts he would turn up looking like a grotesque parody of Bertie Wooster.

Nothing could dissuade Horace from his dream. One day, after he had ordered a dry Martini in the spitting ring of a boozer in Barnsley and received a derisive sneer from the barman, I said to him: 'Look, wouldn't it be easier if you became Freddie Trueman or Len Hutton or someone like that. Someone a bit nearer your own background?' He gave me a sad smile and sipped what in Barnsley passes for a dry Martini. 'My dear Michael, you simply don't understand. This Sheppard chappie stands for everything I envy. Poise, breeding, talent. It's all there, old chap. You can't do better than copy a master, after all,' he said. I knew then it was hopeless, that nothing short of brain surgery would change his fantasy.

On the whole his friends and team mates came to learn how to live with him. The important exception was our captain who had an immense contempt for anyone who couldn't drink fifteen pints without falling down and a firm belief that God had a Yorkshire accent. He treated Horace with an undisguised hostility. The flashpoint in their relationship occurred during a game when they were batting together. We were in need of quick runs, a tactical consideration which Horace placed second to his impersonation of David Sheppard. After playing an elegant on-drive through mid-wicket he maintained the final position, carefully checking that the shot was a perfect replica of Sheppard's and oblivious to the fact that the captain was galloping up and down the wicket like a runaway tram. The captain had completed two runs and was about to set off on a risky third when he suddenly realised that Horace had not moved and was still engrossed in a painstaking survey of his shot.

Our captain inspected the immaculate statue at the other end of the wicket and, after a moment's hesitation, set off towards him. It looked as if he decided there was a run to be had, but I believe he had murder in his mind, that his target was not the opposite crease but a point somewhere between Horace's eyes. At this moment Horace awoke from his reverie, saw the skipper charging down the wicket, saw the ball winging in from the outfield and with an imperious gesture held up his hand and shouted, in what he took to be an upper-class drawl, 'No. Get back, skipper.'

'I'll gi' thi' get back yer great Nancy,' yelled the skipper charging towards him. At which point Horace took the decision which undeniably saved his life. As the skipper closed on him, bat raised, he set off in vain pursuit of the other crease. He was run out by several yards and retired to the pavilion trying to be very public school about it. Our captain went on to make fifty and get a collection, which probably accounted for the fact that he didn't strangle Horace on his return to the pavilion. It was shortly after this incident that Horace had his dreams cruelly and finally shattered. He was by this time so well known in the league that he was a natural target for those fast bowlers whose one reaction to eccentricity of any kind was a well-directed bumper. Horace's ambition to be a gentleman and play at Lord's with his hero was taken from him by a swarthy paceman from Rotherham who distinctly heard Horace say, 'Spiffing shot,' after he had square-cut him to the boundary. The next ball was short of a length and of immense pace. It lifted from the wicket like a missile and struck Horace full in the groin.

As he lay there all pretence left him. He was no longer David Sheppard but Horace from the backs who had been painfully felled. He relieved his agony with a colourful description of the bowler and his family. The language was not the kind you would expect from someone who had read a book on etiquette, nor did the accent signify expensive elocution lessons in Wakefield. At the end of the tirade, our opening bat said to him jokingly, 'The Reverend David Sheppard wouldn't have said that Horace.' Horace looked at him balefully. '. . . . David Sheppard,' he said, simply.

It was the end of his dream and we did our best to console him. He gave up cricket at the end of that season and after a brief period, where he flirted with the idea of being Luis Miguel Dominguin, dropped out of the fantasy business altogether. He had learned the lesson that it is safer to keep your sporting fantasies locked in the mind.

John Willy Jardine

I once played for a team captained by a man who thought he was Douglas Jardine. The fact that his name was John Willy and the team he captained swam in the lower reaches of Yorkshire league cricket did nothing to dissuade the impersonation. He even went to the lengths of buying himself a multicoloured cricket cap of the sort that Jardine favoured, which in the area where we played, constituted an act of unsurpassed bravery. The cap was finally taken from him in the most innocent circumstances, when one Christmas John Willy arrived home from the pit to find it sodden and dejected, sitting atop the snowman erected by his children in their back yard. He was never the same without it.

Of all the captains I have played with he was the most impressive, the hardest, the most imaginative, and I first came across him shortly after leaving school and joining my first league side. In the coal lorry going to the match he explained the subtleties of playing in this particular class of cricket.

'Now tha' sees first thing is t'new ball. There's nowt fancy in this league, we get a new ball every Barnsley Feast so tha' has to be thinking all t'time abart when it might come and how tha' gets thi' hands on it first,' he said. He explained that he was only telling us this because he had heard that the team we were to play that afternoon had bought a new ball recently and he reckoned they were saving it for us. That being the case it was important to the outcome of the game that we get our hands on it first.

We arrived at the ground and were changing when the opposing captain came into our dressing room. He was the local headmaster and therefore not very popular with John Willy who thought teachers were layabouts.

'Good afternoon John Willy, lovely day,' said the headmaster.

John Willy was never a man for pleasantries. 'I hear tha' bought a new ball,' he said. The headmaster smiled blandly. 'You have been misinformed John Willy. This is the match

ball.' He produced a battered piece of leather which looked as
if it had suffered a lifetime being bounced on concrete wickets.
John Willy nodded and said nothing. He went out with the
headmaster, won the toss and elected to bat. As he strapped
his pads on and prepared to open the innings he said to us:

'Yon teacher's trying summat on. Ah reckon he's got t'new
ball in his pocket. If it happens that he brings it out when play
starts, then I want you all to stand down by yon hedge at
square leg. First chance I get I'll thump t'ball down theer and I
don't want it to come back. Understand?' We nodded.

Sure enough, as the opening bowler measured out his run
the headmaster, with a superior smirk handed him a shiny,
red new ball. Halfway through the first over John Willy lay
back and pulled the ball hard towards the square leg boundary
where it crashed into the hedge. After ten minutes of fruitless
searching the umpires, who were worried about the game
running into licensing hours, ordered the headmaster to re-
start the game using the battered old ball we had seen in the
pavilion.

Back in the dressing room someone said, 'Who found it?'
Our slow bowler put his hand up. 'Wheer is it then?' someone
asked. 'Down a bloody rabbit hole' said the slow bowler.
Overjoyed by his tactical triumph, John Willy played an in-
spiring innings, and when we declared with about 160 on the
board he had scored an unbeaten ninety-odd. He came in the
dressing room pink with self-satisfaction. 'That's what tha'
calls strategy,' he said to the room. 'Now then, wheer's t'new
ball.' 'Down a rabbit hole,' said the slow bowler. 'Wheer?'
asked John Willy, his face clouding. The slow bowler repeated
what he had said. John Willy by this time was trying hard to
control himself. Finally he addressed the slow bowler: 'Then
go and get t'bloody thing from t'bloody rabbit hole and polish
it up nice and shiny.'

Mercifully the slow bowler located the rabbit hole and found
the new ball. Polishing it on his backside John Willy went
round to the opposition's dressing room and said to the captain, 'By a stroke of good luck we've managed to find t'proper
match ball. I tek it tha's no objection to us using it.' The
headmaster, aware he had come up against a superior tacti-
cian, shook his head sullenly. Armed with the new ball we got
them all out for less than fifty. 'Strategy, that's what tha' needs

in this game,' John Willy kept saying, and I came to regard him with the kind of hero worship I had reserved up until that time for The Wolf of Kabbul and Baldy Hogan.

I was with him the day he perished and it was a fitting end to such an unorthodox career. John Willy was batting in a local derby game which contained more than the usual amount of needle when he fell victim to one of cricket's more outrageous whims. He snicked a ball very hard on to his body whereupon it somehow burst through the flies of his trousers and settled inside his pants just above his knee. The wicket keeper and the bowler, sensing an easy wicket and undue humiliation for John Willy, set off toward him with the intention of rescuing the ball while John Willy went through an incredible panto-mime trying to extract it and throw it on the ground.

Undeterred by John Willy's dire warnings about what might happen to them if they laid a finger on him, the wicket keeper and the fast bowler both made a purposeful approach toward their victim. What happened next is a matter for dispute. Some say John Willy chinned the fast bowler with a left hook, some say the fast bowler knocked himself out by running on to John Willy's elbow just as the batsman was extracting the ball. Whatever the circumstances, the fast bowler lost two front teeth and spent the next five minutes flat on his back, his

'*John Willy was given out for "ungentlemanly" conduct*'

42

thoughts a million miles from the cricket field. Eventually John Willy was given out for 'ungentlemanly conduct' and the fast bowler taken to the local infirmary for a check up. Soon after John Willy was called before the disciplinary committee and severely reprimanded.

The following Christmas he found his cap on the snowman and being the sort of man who could read the signs better than most he retired. We gave him a presentation dinner the following season and the chairman of the club, while handing him a chromium plated cake stand, described him as a 'great captain and a gentleman'. We were not sure how John Willy would react to being called a 'gentleman', but he took it very well. Nor did he disagree with being called a 'great captain'. What he said was, 'Me and D. R. Jardine played it t'same way.' So far as I know Douglas Jardine never chinned a fast bowler, but we all knew what John Willy meant.

Anything Goes

To have played cricket and never taken part in a knock-out competition is like joining the Army and never hearing a shot fired in anger. Knock-out cricket is designed to bring the worst out of players and spectators alike. It gives off that most delicious of cricket perfumes: the heady whiff of crushed grass and skullduggery.

My old man adored knock-out cricket. Being the sort of player who could turn a gentle game of beach cricket into something resembling the landing at Iwo Jima he relished the tense and often violent atmosphere of knock-out cricket. Much of the excitement at these games comes from the spectators whose normal ration of pride in the local team is supplemented by the fact that they have ten bob on the game with the local bookie.

My old man told a lovely story of the time he played his first knock-out game. His father was a big betting man and was well pleased when the opposition was bowled out for 42.

It seemed a walkover for my old man's team, so much so that when he went to look at the batting order the skipper had only put down four names and said to my dad: 'Off tha' goes Sammy. We shan't need thee.'

Fortunately he stuck around long enough to see his team collapse to the extent that when he went out to bat at No. 11 his side were 20 for 9 wickets and needed 23 to win. As he went down the pavilion steps he was the object of much excellent advice from the betting fraternity, none more pithy than that offered by his father, who said, 'If tha' gets out before we've beaten them I'll thump thee ear'ole.'

Basing his innings on this sound advice my old man managed to keep his end up while the batsman at the other end scored the runs to win the game.

The rejoicing was great and my old man was later downing a hero's pint in a nearby hostelry when he was approached by a local who said:

'Spending thi' collection money then, Sammy?'

'What collection?' said my old man.

'That what thi' father organised after tha'd won t'game for us. Collected about five quid on thi' behalf.'

Father swallowed his pint and dashed to the ground where he met his old man lurching gently away from the bar.

'Where's my collection then?' he said.

'Supped it' said his old man, burping loudly.

It would be wrong to assume however that knock-out cricket only affects the spectators. It is beautifully designed to corrupt everyone who comes in contact with it.

In the knock-out cricket I used to play in, the right to cheat your way to victory was not written in the laws but it was certainly branded deep into the soul of every player. The rules allowed each team to play two professionals which meant that every team went to extraordinary lengths to play as many professionals as they could without their opponents finding out. As local professionals were well known the illegal ones had to be imported from nearby towns. When I played in these games they used to give the illicit professionals false names.

All this changed the year that the winning team was found to comprise of two Browns, four Smiths and five Jones. A subsequent inquiry revealed they were all professionals from the Lancashire League with names like Leatherbarrow and Strongitharm. After that the rules were changed and the teams had to declare the correct names of their players before the competition started. But there were ways round that. Once we arrived to play a team in the semi-final and the opposing captain popped into our dressing-room just before the game started to say he was a man short. 'Can I borrow a substitute, Fred,' he asked our skipper. 'No,' he replied, helpfully.

The opposing skipper then asked if he could pick a substitute from the spectators, and Fred agreed only if he had the right to veto. They set off round the ground together looking for likely prospects. Every time the opposing captain indicated a husky young lad Fred, who was enjoying himself immensely, would shake his head and point to an old man in a wheel chair. They had made a complete circuit of the ground and reached the pavilion again when the opposing captain pointed to a hunched, wizened figure sitting on the grass.

An Indian wearing a bus conductor's uniform. Our captain thought this was a huge joke.

'They've got Gunga Din playing for them,' he told us. Someone reminded him cautiously that Indians could play cricket. 'But he's a bus conductor not Ranjitsinhji,' he replied. He received the first inkling of the way in which he had been deceived when we batted. After a couple of overs the little Indian was asked to bowl which was a bit strange considering they had found him on the ground only ten minutes earlier. We had our suspicions confirmed in the Indian's first over which contained five leg breaks and one googly of a quality normally reserved for Test batsmen. From that moment we knew our captain had been tricked and that we were doomed. The Indian took eight wickets for less than 20 and we lost the match.

Our skipper was fit for nothing after the game. He wasn't angry, just disappointed that he had not been the first to invent such a stunning piece of twisting. He just sat in the bar downing pints of bitter and staring moodily at the floor. But his worst moment was yet to come. The little Indian, back in his bus conductor's uniform, was sitting across the room with the winning team when someone asked him, just to rub it in, who was the best batsman he had bowled to. Everyone on our side stopped talking and listened because we still didn't know who or what he was.

Our skipper burped wittily and said sarcastically, 'Bradman.' 'No,' said the Indian, 'I think Len Hutton was the best.' It was too much for the skipper. He gave all his gear away and swore he would never play again. We never did find out who that little Indian was.

What we did learn, however, those of us reared on knock-out cricket was that while it is perfectly true that the game can uplift the spirit and make men angels it can also stimulate the darkest corners of a man's personality and turn him into a criminal mastermind.

Brotherly Love

I used to play cricket with a man called Billy Hopkinson who made Nastase look like the best behaved athlete in the world. Whenever he was given out LBW his team-mates would evacuate the dressing-room taking all their gear with them before Billy returned to vent his rage on whatever he could put his hands on. The main sufferers were the unfortunate batsmen who were at the crease when Billy was given out.

All they could do was stand and watch as their gear came through the dressing-room window to be followed by Billy's gear, the wooden benches, the matting floor carpet and, on very bad days, the large brown teapot that the tea ladies borrowed from the Church Hall and which was only used for funerals and cricket matches.

As befitted a world class tantrum-thrower, Billy Hopkinson could produce an outburst at the correct tactical time. He was the best ooher and aaher I ever played with and also the best running commentator.

On arriving at the wicket the new batsman would find Billy staring thoughtfully at a spot just short of a length. 'Looks nasty to me that does,' he'd say, sometimes going on his hands and knees to calculate the size of an imaginary ridge.

'I've never fancied this wicket since Albert got his nose broke. Made a right mess it did. You could hear the crack a mile away. Off a slow bowler, too,' he would say while the batsman tried to look cool.

From that point on the batsman's survival depended on his ability to concentrate on a game while being subjected to a barrage of propaganda from Billy at first slip. Any ball that went past the bat would bring an anguished 'Ooooh' or 'Aaaah' from Billy. It didn't matter if it was a yard outside the off stump, Billy reacted as if it had passed through the wickets.

Not surprisingly Billy wasn't the most popular cricketer in the district. There were many players who disliked having been bowled out while in the middle of an argument with Billy about whether or not the previous ball had shaved the wickets.

One player dismissed in such a manner decided on swift justice and instead of returning to the pavilion set off after Billy waving his bat like a club. But Billy was soon three fields away and he wisely took no further part in the game, spending the afternoon at home and sending his missus down to the ground for his kit.

I only saw him beaten at his own game once and that was by a dark, squat little man who answered everything Billy said about him with a tiny smile, a neat bow of the head and a 'Thank you very much.' Finally Billy could endure it no longer.

At the end of the over he confronted the batsman: 'Ayup mister. I've been talking to thee all afternoon and tha's said nowt. What's up?' The batsman looked at him, smiled, bowed and said: 'Thank you very much.' Billy turned in despair to the other batsman. 'What the bloody hell's up wi' thi' mate,' he said.

'Didn't tha' know Billy? He doesn't speak English. He's Polish,' the batsman said.

'Polish!' said Billy. 'Polish! What's a bloody Polisher doing playing cricket?'

He was silent for the rest of the afternoon, only occasionally muttering the odd obscenity about foreigners. It never occurred to him that there was something very odd about a Pole who spoke no English and yet played cricket well. He was too busy fuming to consider that he might have been conned by a superior foe.

None of us dare put the point to him and indeed we were glad we didn't for otherwise we should have missed those marvellous moments in subsequent matches when after giving a new batsman the ritual spiel he would look at him and say: 'I suppose tha' speaks English lad?'

Normally his tantrums were designed to win a cricket match but once he lost one with a display of temperament which was spectacular even by his own high standards.

An occasional member of the team was Billy's brother, the aforesaid Albert who was reputed to have had his nose broken by a slow bowler. Whatever brotherly love they might have had for one another they kept well hidden on the cricket field. Billy believed Albert was useless and Albert's opinion of Billy was unprintable. The more tense the game, the more bitter became the feeling between them.

Their loathing of one another boiled over in one game when Albert was bowling the final over against the last two batsmen of the opposing side who wanted four to win. The very last ball of the game was struck by the number eleven straight to brother Billy who dropped the catch. Albert stood, hands on hips, glowering at his errant brother. 'You great twerp,' he bellowed. Billy, by now purple with embarrassment at having dropped the catch and enraged by his brother, shouted back:

'Tha' don't deserve wickets bowling bloody long 'ops like that.'

'Don't make excuses. I could have copped that in mi' gob. Tha' couldn't catch pneumonia,' said Albert.

This proved too much for Billy. Picking up the ball he advanced on his brother. 'If tha' so good at catching let's see thi' stop this one,' he said. He was about four yards from Albert when he threw the ball with all his considerable power. Wisely Albert ducked and the ball went for four overthrows and we had lost the match.

Billy and Albert were still arguing as we went back to the dressing rooms. Later they went behind the pavilion for a fight and were still at it when we left the ground. They both retired soon after that and went to barrack Yorkshire sitting at opposite ends of Bramall Lane.

Some years later I was reminded of Billy when I was playing for Barnsley against a team which contained a character renowned for his tantrums and his gamesmanship. He was a quick bowler and particularly rough on young players. He was bowling against us in one match and doing well both as a talker and a bowler until our number five batsman came to the wicket.

He was a young spindly lad with National Health spectacles and a bat which seemed several sizes too large for him. As he took guard the fast bowler commenced the treatment. 'Sending in short-sighted dwarfs to play us now. Must be short of players,' he shouted to the wicket-keeper.

His first ball was a good one a shade short outside the off stump. The batsman went on the back foot, the bat flashed and the bowler was left speechless as the ball sped to the boundary. It was the shot of a class batsman. The bowler turned to me and said ruefully: 'Not bad, not bad. What's his name?'

'Boycott, Geoffrey Boycott,' I said.

Tales Worth Telling

At the very beginning of *Close of Play*, by Neville Cardus, there is a cartoon by that talented man, Bernard Hollowood. It shows two boys standing before a wall with stumps chalked on it. One is a ragamuffin, the other bespectacled and bookish. The latter is saying to the rapscallion, 'No, you be Len Hutton. I'll be Neville Cardus.'

Although my eyesight is perfect, and not even my best friend could describe me as widely read, I have always associated myself with the bookworm in the cartoon. I wouldn't have minded being Len Hutton, but I would have sold my soul to have been blessed with Sir Neville's gifts.

I still find it difficult to believe his confession that most of those marvellous quotes he attributes to the cricketers he wrote about were invented. And yet I was prepared to do so, because I heard the same statement from his own lips the one and only time I met him.

We lunched together, and because at the time I was gathering material for an article about Wilfred Rhodes, I asked him the source of one of my favourite anecdotes about Wilfred which Sir Neville had written. The story concerns Charles McGahey, the old Essex player, going out to bat on a sunny day at Bramall Lane, Sheffield. As he walked out to face Rhodes the weather changed. Looking over his shoulder at the darkening sun and anticipating a sticky wicket, McGahey said 'Ullo! McGahey caught Tunnicliffe bowled Rhodes . . . O.' And so it was, both innings.

Sir Neville smiled at the memory and then said, disarmingly, 'Oh, I made it up.' It was my first traumatic experience. He went on to explain that his job was to write scripts for the cricketers who, in the main, were unable to say what they undoubtedly would have said had they possessed Sir Neville's imagination. As he expounded his theory, he must have seen the look of disappointment on my face.

'You mustn't worry, young man, because it happens to be true,' he said.

'What was true?' I asked, somewhat baffled.

'McGahey caught Tunnicliffe bowled Rhodes both innings,' said Sir Neville, as if that explained everything.

Sir Neville's confession raises the whole question of the validity of the sporting anecdote. I once asked Fred Trueman, who has been the subject of more stories than any cricketer in the history of the game, how many were true. 'About ten per cent,' he said.

He didn't mind the majority of them – indeed, he was flattered – but there were one or two he could do without. The story he really objected to, and has spent a lifetime trying to deny, was the one about him sitting next to a high dignitary of the Indian Government at dinner, digging him in the ribs and saying: 'Ayup Gunga Din, pass t'salt.'

All that Fred's denials have achieved is another punch-line to the story whereby the teller states that when asked about the yarn's validity, Fred said: 'It's a lie. I never said that. It were t'chutney I were after.'

Although that particular story was an original in that it was invented especially for Fred, quite a few of the others he inherited from the folk-lore of fast bowlers. The one about Fred objecting to a 'fancy hat' cocking a toe at him and, after sufficient warning, dropping a 90 mph yorker on the offending article, was told about Kortright, as well as Larwood, before Fred inherited it.

In the Kortright version the bowler is alleged to have told the batsman that he allowed only one batsman to lift his toe at him, and that was W. G. Grace. The batsman declined the advice and was carried from the field.

In the Larwood/Trueman version, the stricken batsman falls to the floor in anguish. Fieldsmen gather round and remove pad, sock and boot and solicitously massage the bruised foot. After much palaver, the batsman is able to replace his gear and stand up. As he picks up his bat and prepares to continue, Harold/Fred, who has been watching the performance says:

'Are tha' alreet young feller?'

'Yes, thank you very much,' says the batsman.

'Can tha' walk?'

'I think so, thank you.'

'Good. Well, get thissen off to t'pavilion because tha'rt LBW,' says Harold/Fred.

A lovely story, but Fred denies it, and I'll bet it never happened to Larwood nor to Kortright. It doesn't really matter because as Sir Neville always believed, cricketers should concentrate on what they do best and leave the legends to those whose job it is to invent them.

An interesting variation on that story concerns Arthur Wood, wicket-keeper in the great Yorkshire side of the thirties. Yorkshire were playing one of the universities and were having their ambition to get home on the second day slightly thwarted by the elegant defence of some young buck. At the start of an over bowled by the great Hedley Verity, Wood decided to take matters in hand. After every ball he would say to the batsman: 'Well played, young sir', or 'Fine shot, young man', so that by the sixth ball of the over the batsman was so convinced of his own mastery that he advanced down the wicket preparatory to hitting Verity out of sight. As he did so he heard Wood say:

'Tha's missed it young man. Now p— off, we've got a train to catch.'

I asked Fred to tell me a true story himself, and he recounted a bizarre incident which happened on his one and only tour of India for the Royal Cricket Association's Silver Jubilee matches. According to Fred, he was enduring a long and gruelling journey when the train made a stop at a tiny station a million miles from nowhere. Fred decided to stretch his legs and, wandering on to the platform, met the stationmaster. The official was delighted at meeting the great man, and was overjoyed when Fred asked him where the toilets were.

He insisted on taking Fred into the station buildings and into a room where – and Fred avows this to be true – he drew back a curtain and unveiled a Victorian chamber pot which had F. S. Trueman written on it.

How the railwayman knew that one day F. S. Trueman would step off a train at his station and, moreover, want to use his toilet, is a story beyond the imaginings of a Cardus. How long he had waited, and what gave him the idea, no one knows. What happened to the chamber pot, whether it occupies pride of place in the stationmaster's trophy cabinet, or has become a monument of historical interest for the tourist trade, we shall likely never know.

'Is that a true story, F.S.?' I asked.

'Would I tell you a lie, Parky, my old son?' he said.

I didn't answer. They knighted Sir Neville for his embellishments, and by the same token I reckon that if Fred was having me on, he ought to get the Pulitzer Prize for Literature. Moreover, if it is fiction and it passes into the Trueman mythology, Fred will have the supreme satisfaction of knowing that at least one of the lies told about him was his own invention.

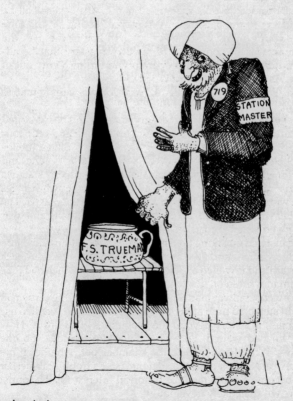

'he drew back a curtain and unveiled a Victorian chamber pot'

Cricket Characters

I remember going to see Nottinghamshire play Yorkshire when I was a lad. It must have been some time ago because Notts had a good team in those days and bowed the knee to no one. If memory is true the game was played at Bramall Lane and Nottinghamshire won the toss and batted. What I do remember clearly is that Notts opened with Keeton and Harris. Now they were a formidable pair, and Harris was not only a fine player but a man with an impish way of doing things.

He was in the habit of opening proceedings by hanging a 'Do Not Disturb' sign on his bails before taking first ball, and like a few of the greats Notts players – Gunn, Hardstaff and Simpson – was a player of infinite mood and zest. That day long ago he decided to bait the large and partisan Yorkshire crowd by demonstrating in the morning session the art of defensive play. He hardly scored a run before lunch and the louder the crowd booed the more grandiose became his defensive flourishes. He went to lunch on a fanfare of catcalls.

After lunch he took Yorkshire apart and finished up with a double century treating the crowd to a doff of the cap and a sweeping bow whenever, and however reluctantly, they applauded one magnificent shot after the other.

Modern-day cricketers could well argue that nowadays a pre-lunch sleep-in such as Harris promoted would have the pavilion burnt down and the square buried in beer cans. And they might be right because if it be true that on the whole today's cricketers have lost the grand manner of rebuking their critics, it is for certain that today's crowds have similarly lost the art of telling the players where to get off.

Arthur 'Ticker' Mitchell, who ruined many a Roses game for a Lancastrian, will bear witness to this. He was playing in a Yorkshire *v* Lancashire game at Old Trafford and doing his duty by staying there and scoring nothing when play was interrupted by a voice from the popular side.

'Mitchell,' the voice yelled, in aggrieved tones. 'Mitchell, I want tha' to know that every Bank Holiday I come here to see t' cricket and every Bank Holiday, bare none, tha' comes out and buggers it up for me. Mitchell, I've had enough, I'm going home and I'm not coming back . . . ever.'

The saddest decline in modern cricket is the relationship between opposing teams. During MCC's recent games against Australia we have heard much of the 'verbalizing' that goes on during the Test matches, and, although we only get the expurgated version there can be little doubt that the on-field chat between the players is not that which passed for pertinent, or proper, when W. G. was in his pomp.

The point is, of course, that today's bad-mouth brigade are incapable of understanding the nuance of the oblique statement. Take a straightforward example. Today's batsman is likely greeted with the news that the opposing quickie is going to knock his f...... head off. A few years ago things were different.

My old man told a story of playing against a fast bowler of exceptional pace. After the first over when my old man literally did not see one delivery he confided to the stumper, 'By heck, but yon bloke's quick.'

'True,' said the stumper, 'but tha' should have seen him before he were gassed.'

But the best example of psychological warfare in cricket concerns the elderly judge playing for the local village side. The opening batsman of the opposing team hit the ball into the rhododendrons at square leg and the judge trotted off in pursuit. He disappeared into the bushes and about three minutes elapsed before he emerged with the ball.

At tea the judge seemed broody, and to break his mood the skipper gently kidded him about being long in the bushes.

'What kept you?' he asked.

'Well, to tell the truth when I went into the rhododendrons to retrieve the ball I came upon a couple making love. I had to ask them to move over in order to get the ball. Most distressing,' said the judge.

'Oh, come now,' said the skipper, 'you're a man of the world. Surely you're not upset at seeing two people making love.'

'It's not that at all,' said the judge. 'It did not upset me seeing the fellow on the job – but I must confess I was very upset when the bounder came in at number seven.'

'I went into the rhododendrons to retrieve the ball . . .'

Present-day cricketers could learn much from that true story. The moral is there are more ways of getting at the crowd and your opponents than giving the V-sign. Perhaps all is not lost. Not long ago Harvey-Walker, the Derbyshire batsman, announced his opinion of a brutal wicket at Buxton by striding to the middle and handing over his false teeth to the square leg umpire. He was out in rapid fashion whereupon, with massive dignity, he collected his molars and replaced them in his mouth, before making his way back to the pavilion.

I think Harvey-Walker would have loved playing with Mr Harris who never overstepped the line dividing good-natured teasing of your opponents and bad-tempered abuse. Sometimes, during a long innings – and he played many for Notts – the game would be interrupted while a minion bearing a telegram addressed to Harris and marked 'Most Urgent' walked to the wicket.

Harris would open the telegram, read it, dismiss the messenger and resume play against opponents much disconcerted by the unusual interruption and consumed with curiosity as to the contents of a telegram so urgent it had to be delivered to a fellow on a cricket field.

Had they inquired of the recipient the nature of the message they would have found it read: 'WELL DONE SO FAR BUT KEEP GOING YOU FOOL, signed C. HARRIS.' Sending telegrams to himself was not a mark of Harris's eccentricity, rather a demonstration of his belief that of all games cricket is the one best suited to the man of wit and style and a plague on the oafs and dullards.

The Wars of the Roses

There is no more certain indication of the decline of cricket as a popular spectator sport than the pathetic attendance at the present day Roses game. Once these were glorious encounters as important as test matches played to full houses and the noise of battle on and off the field.

The fact of the matter is that today, except for a few nostalgics like myself, the prospect of a Roses game quickens as many pulses in Leeds and Manchester as the news that the Turkish Bank Rate has been increased to 6½%. Today the Wars of the Roses is a tired headline to sell a story that people stopped reading a long time ago.

It still meant something in 1947 when I went to my first Roses game. We queued for three hours outside Bramall Lane, Sheffield, and in that blessed moment when I was jostled through the turnstile, I felt as if I had arrived in Paradise. We sat on the hard concrete terracing of the football ground, knees drawn up under our chins, arms pinioned by one's neighbours, and there we remained for the next eight hours in a state of acute physical discomfort sustained only by the knowledge that this was no ordinary cricket match.

To stand up to relieve cramped muscles was to invite an apple core or a pork pie crust to the back of the head along with the usual polite advice to 'Sit thissen down Gladys.'

The Bramall Lane crowd has never been in sympathy with the physical discomfort of others. A few seasons later I was sitting on the same piece of concrete watching Yorkshire play Middlesex. It was during Compton's golden days when his face shone from every hoarding advertising hair dressing. In Yorkshire, among the rank and file cricket supporters, at least, there was always a guarded attitude toward Compton. He was too flash for their tastes, too much of a fly boy. Brylcreem and cricket don't mix in Yorkshire.

On this particular occasion Compton was granted a privileged insight into the way that the cricket lovers of Sheffield feel about the suffering of their fellow men. Yorkshire were batting when play was held up by the appearance on the field of what is called a Sheffield mongrel, which is to say a dog of exceedingly dubious parentage. The dog careered around the field defying the energetic attempts of the Middlesex side to catch it. It should be explained at this point that the sympathies of the Yorkshire crowd were entirely with the Middlesex men, it being a commonly held view in Yorkshire that dogs are for racing and not for petting.

Eventually it was Compton who caught it. It had to be, it was his year. He swooped low as the dog raced past him and scooped it triumphantly aloft. The crowd was relieved that the game could go on but remained unimpressed by Compton's panache. Still brandishing the dog Compton trotted towards the pavilion and as he did so the creature, being born in Sheffield and therefore no respecter of personalities, bit him smartly on the arm. Compton dropped the animal and stood rubbing the bite. The huge crowd watched the performance dispassionately and then someone from the football terraces shouted 'Put some bloody Brylcreem on it Compton.'

I digress only to acquaint you with my neighbours on that lovely Saturday in 1947 when I saw my first Roses game. There was a roar as Sellers, broad as a muck stack, won the toss and chose to bat. In the opening over I caught the sense of tradition and meaning that set these games apart and made them special. There was an atmosphere, a tenseness about the play which I have never tasted since, not even in a Test match. When Yorkshire lost their first wicket with only twelve scored the ground was in mourning. There came to the wicket an unknown called Smithson playing in his first Roses game.

In a situation calling for trench warfare Smithson decided on a cavalry charge. No one who sat in Bramall Lane that day could forget his innings. By any standards it was a good one, but in the context of the grim Roses games it was sensational. He defied tradition by hitting three fours and a three in one over, he made old men wince with his daring strokeplay and when he was out two short of his century every spectator creaked to his feet and applauded.

In his excellent book *The Wars of the Roses* the late and very lamented A. A. Thomson recalls the innings and tells how, before Smithson went in to bat Emmott Robinson told him: 'Na, lad, what tha' has to do is shove thi' bat in t'block-hole and keep it there, chose 'ow.' When Smithson was out for 98 and with the cheers of the crowd still warming his ears, Emmott sought him out and reprimanded him for his 'outrageous levity.' At the end of the telling off Emmott was seen to shake his head despairingly and mutter, 'We'll never learn that lad.'

At the end of the day as we streamed out of grimy Bramall Lane, a scruffy, jostling, happy crowd, I felt privileged to have been initiated into cricket's most secret ritual. Warmed by the presence of 30,000 others I felt part of a tradition that would last for ever no matter what became of the rest of the game. In fact I was in at the beginning of the end. The tradition of the Roses game has not been enough to protect it from cricket's present maladies. What was once a meaningful occasion is nowadays just another three-day match.

A few years ago I went to Old Trafford for the Roses game. The morning sun shone, Old Trafford was beautiful, Trueman had his tail up, the Yorkshire fielding was of the highest and all these treasures were witnessed by a crowd so small it might have arrived in one double-decker bus. My mind drifted back to Sheffield in 1947 and I would willingly in that moment have swopped my seat in the stand for that concrete step if it meant a taste of the old excitement. I pitied any young boy being blooded that day at Old Trafford. His head full of dreams and Cardus beforehand, he must have felt bitterly let down by what he saw.

In the bar I tried to start an argument but no one wanted to know. Completely disenchanted I found myself a lonely place in the sun and sat there sulking. Nothing altered my mood, not even the fact that at close of play Yorkshire were well on top. I went home knowing that things would never be the same again, that to recapture what used to be I must now rely on memory, Sir Neville and my old man. The consolation is that tradition dies harder with the players than the spectators and this fact at least will ensure that what happens in the middle during a Roses match will continue to be very different from the sort of thing that happens in any other kind of cricket match. The players of both counties are sufficiently well versed in their heritage to regard the Roses games as something special no matter how large the public apathy. I cherish one story told me by that fine Yorkshire cricketer Ken Taylor, now coaching abroad, that accounts for the reason why the Roses game will always be held to be different by the players. Taylor's first game against Lancashire was at Old Trafford. Yorkshire were doing badly as he walked down the pavilion steps on his way to the wicket. The Lancashire crowd was baying for blood. As he approached the pavilion gate it was opened for him by a uniformed attendant who, as Ken passed, politely saluted and then said out of the corner of his mouth: 'Best of luck lad, but think on, don't be long.'

Taylor was still bemused by this quote as he took guard. Unfortunately he was bowled first ball. He made his way sadly and slowly back to the pavilion. At the gate the same man was waiting. He opened the gate, touched his forelock and said: 'Thank you lad.'

Those Who Stand and Serve

I remember my first umpire well. His name was Jim Smith and he always took his teeth out before a game. I never discovered why but I always supposed it was a safety precaution due to the state of our wickets and the ferocity of our cricket.

He was a marvellous man, tall and dignified even without his teeth, with an infallible technique for puncturing swollen heads. I remember as a youngster playing well and scoring fifty or so in a game he was umpiring. I carried my bat and as I came off the field, triumphant, imagining myself to be an unbelievable mixture of Bradman and Hutton, he joined me at my shoulder. As we walked in together, I looked towards him anticipating a word of praise. He glanced sidelong at me and out of the corner of his mouth said: 'Does tha' want some advice, lad?'

I said I did.

'Well get thi' bloody hair cut,' he said.

Two matches later he gave me out LBW and as I walked sullenly past him he said, out of the same corner of his toothless mouth:

'If tha'd get thi' bloody hair cut tha'd stop them balls wi' thi' bat.'

Jim Smith was my introduction to that delightful body of men: the cricket umpire. I can think of no other group that does so much for so little. By comparison the soccer referee is a pampered ninny, and the fact that cricket has survived this far without requiring the umpires to take the field carrying truncheons says much for their character. The secret of course lies in their humour. There are few funny stories about soccer or Rugby referees and anyone who tells me a funny story about a tennis umpire will receive a gold plated pig by return of post. But there is a Bumper Fun Book of Funny Cricket Umpire Stories.

Many of them concern Alec Skelding. My favourite Skelding story concerns the aggrieved batsman who, on being given out LBW, addressed Skelding thus:

'Where's your white stick umpire?'

'Left it at home,' said Alec.

'What about your guide dog,' said the batsman.

'Got rid of it for yappin' same as I'm getting rid of you,' replied Skelding.

Joe Hayes never rose to Skelding's heights in cricket but in the local league I played in as a youth he was just as big a legend. Those who knew Joe well, always appealed for everything as opening time approached because Joe had a job as a waiter in a local boozer and had to be on duty at 6 p.m. It was his proud boast that he had never been late at the boozer for 20 years and could produce several hundred cursing batsmen to bear him witness. His other quirk was a dislike of loud appealing. He himself rarely raised his voice above a murmur and his face creased in pain and disgust whenever a bowler bellowed in his earhole.

We had in our team at the time the best appealer of all time. His voice rattled windows several miles away and set dogs to whimpering. This particular game his raucous appeals eventually got on Joe's nerves. After one particularly loud one Joe could stand it no longer.

'Owz that,' bellowed the bowler.

'Not out,' Joe bellowed back in an even louder voice. The bowler stood amazed that Joe should raise his voice.

'I'm only bloody askin' thi',' he said in a pained tone.

'Ay and I'm only bloody tellin' thi',' shouted Joe.

All of which leads to Cec Pepper who as a player in the Lancashire League was renowned as much for his verbal battles with umpires as he was for his cricketing prowess.

Pepper was the scourge of Lancashire League umpires, blasting the meek with his belligerent appealing, making the lay preachers blush with his vivid language. The umpire who faced up to him had to be a special kind of human being and George Long was such a man.

George was standing one day at the end where Pepper was bowling, when Pepper made one of his raucous Australian appeals for LBW, which was answered by a quiet 'Not out.' Whereupon Pepper gave vent to a histrionic stream of invective, throwing in all the stock-in-trade props – spectacles, white stick, guide dog, illegitimacy, bloody-minded Englishness, and four-letter words: all of which George completely ignored.

The same thing happened after the next ball and yet again the following one, after which George called 'Over' and walked to his square leg position, followed by Pepper – obviously disturbed by the lack of reaction from the umpire.

'I suppose you're going to report all this bad language to the League?' said Pepper.

'No' replied George. 'Ah likes a chap as speaks his mind.' Pepper was obviously delighted.

'So do I,' he said smiling, 'and I must say it's a refreshing change to meet an umpire like you. I'm glad that we understand each other.'

'Aye,' said George.

The first ball of the next over again hit the batsman's pad, whereupon Cec whirled round to George, arms outstretched and did his usual Red Indian war whoop. 'Howzat' was heard all round the ground.

'Not out, you fat Australian bastard,' said George quietly.

Cricket Love Story

I was in my mid-teens and daft as a brush when I met Big Jack. From the moment I first saw him I worshipped him with all the pimply fervour of the adolescent. Looking back now, I realize he was that most pathetic of figures – the good athlete gone to seed.

He had been a marvellous cricketer, a quick bowler blessed with real pace and hostility, a crowd-pleasing thumper of a cricket ball and the safest catcher in the outfield I have ever seen. He would have walked into the county side except for a liking for strong drink and a passion for gambling on the game which would have given them a purple rash at Lord's.

Again, looking back, I can't imagine why I worshipped him so. He wasn't what you would call a 'nice' man. He was selfish, coarse, arrogant, quick-tempered and completely intolerant of anyone who fell below his own high standards on a cricket field. Yet he was good to me.

At the nets he took pains to correct my faults, in the middle he nursed me through my first season of big league cricket peppering my education with unforgettable advice.

Once, after I had been caught out on the square-leg boundary from a long hop, he asked me why I had played the shot. 'I don't know, it just came naturally,' I mumbled. He looked at me sadly. 'What's bloody natural about getting thissen out?' he asked.

There then followed a ten-minute demonstration of how to hit to leg, turning the bat over the ball at the point of impact, pulling it on the carpet through mid-wicket instead of belting it down deep square leg's throat.

He concluded the session by saying, 'I suppose tha' were trying to hit a six?' I nodded. 'Tha' looks like a famine victim,' he said. 'Tha' wants to get thi' mam to change her butcher afore tha' starts hitting sixes.'

He wasn't always so kindly. Anyone dropping a catch from his bowling knew what it was like to be publicly executed. He was no respecter of rank. A young curate fresh from Cambridge, briefly in our area to see how the other half lived, cut short his stay after being blasted by Big Jack on consecutive Saturdays.

Rupert, the chairman's son, downy cheeked from boarding school, who played during his holidays was another victim. He hated Rupert and the feeling was mutual. It wasn't fair because Rupert, for all his faults – and he had many – was a fine player. Their relationship deteriorated into open warfare during a cup game.

We needed about 160 to win and batted like Jessies, all except Rupert, who carried his bat. When he had made 50, I was surprised to see Big Jack go round with the hat for the collection. Perhaps, I thought, Big Jack wants to make it up. I should have known better. We needed about 30 to win when I went in.

Big Jack stopped me at the dressing-room door. 'Tha's better stop there or I'll kick thi' arse,' he said. 'I'll try,' I said. I got done third ball. We lost by 20 runs and Rupert made about 80 not out.

When we had changed, Rupert said. 'Let's go and drink my collection.' We looked at Big Jack. 'It's gone,' he said.

'Where?' asked Rupert.

'T' bookie's got it,' said Jack.

'How much?'

'About eight quid.'

'I see.'

'I'll pay thi' back next week,' said Big Jack.

'No matter,' said Rupert and walked out.

I suppose that was the beginning of the end for Big Jack. He wasn't the same player over the next couple of seasons. He blustered and criticised as much as ever but we didn't take that much notice. What he had done was unforgivable, and he couldn't find it in himself to say he was sorry. Over the two years the team became less and less dependent on him.

We had a new young quick bowler called Arthur, who started to make a name for himself and all of us could see that Big Jack was being eased out. If Big Jack knew, he didn't let on. In the dressing-room, if not on the field, he was still the best bloody cricketer in the county. More than that, he was also the most irresistible male since Valentino popped his clogs.

Big Jack's stories of his sexual adventures were both out-rageous and sad. They were blatant, technicolour lies but the sadness was not so much that we were supposed to believe them but that he grew to believe them himself.

We used to play a game with him. While we were changing we would introduce into the conversation an invented name. For instance someone would say, 'I met a nice bird in a boozer last week. Audrey Gillespie, I think she called herself.' Immediately Big Jack would intervene. 'Audrey Gillespie? I know her. Big Audrey? Oh say, I've had her, tha' know . . .' Then would follow a lurid detailed account of how he and Audrey Gillespie had an affair.

God knows where he got his inspiration from, but on the spur of the moment he would invent ten minutes of dialogue recounting how he and Audrey made it in a bath of rose-scented water while the butler served champagne and a con-cealed orchestra played 'Lovely to Look At'. He couldn't know that one day his fantasies would be turned against him in the cruellest possible way.

It happened at the end of what turned out to be his last season. We went down into the bar at the end of the game and were downing a few when this gorgeous looking girl came into the bar. She bought a port and lemon and sat by herself in a corner.

'I think I know her,' said Big Jack, which was par for the course.

'Out of your class,' said Arthur.

'What's tha' mean? Did I ever tell you about the time I had it off wi' this Duchess I met at Bridlington?' said Big Jack.

'You did,' said Arthur.

Rupert came over. I was surprised to see him because he normally drank with a different school and had barely spoken to Big Jack since the incident with the collection.

'You're a gambling man, Big Jack,' he said. Big Jack nodded.

'Bet you can't pull that girl who's just come in,' said Rupert.

'What's it worth?' asked Big Jack.

'I believe you owe me some money. Let's say if you make it I'll call it quits,' said Rupert.

'Done,' said Big Jack.

He swaggered across the room, his demob suit shiny with age, and plonked himself next to the girl. Next thing he's ordering port and lemon like it's tap water.

'Easy,' he said as he came to the bar for the fifth time. Later she left by herself. Big Jack told us with relish she was a film starlet from London up to see her granny who'd fallen downstairs and broken her leg. 'Did you pull her?' asked Arthur. 'No problem,' said Big Jack. 'Outside t'bus station cafe tomorrow at seven. Like shelling peas.'

He left soon after. 'Need to save myself for tomorrow,' he said.

'He did well,' I said to Rupert, when he'd gone.

'He ought to. I set him up,' he said.

'I don't understand,' I said.

'It's very elaborate really. I paid the girl to come here tonight. I told her to be nice to Big Jack,' he said.

'Why?' I asked.

He looked at me sadly. 'Because I don't like him,' he said.

It nagged me all the way home. I couldn't stop thinking about it. What was the plot? Was she a fella in disguise? Alternatively was she a karate expert who was going to break his neck or worse if he tried anything on?

Next day I caught the bus to town and stood across the street from the bus station cafe. Just before seven o'clock Big Jack arrived, shining like a guardsman's cap badge.

Stood up.

At 7.15 he had bought a paper and was pretending to read it. By 7.40 he had walked round the bus station ten times, wondering if he had got the time and place wrong. I wanted to go and tell him but I couldn't. How do you explain to your hero that he's been stood up? At eight o'clock he jacked it in. He crumpled his paper and I watched him board the bus for home.

That was bad enough, but worse was yet to come. The following Saturday when we were changing, Rupert said, 'How did you make out, Big Jack?'

'What's tha' talking about?' he said.

'The blonde girl you had the date with. What happened?'

'Oh, her. Great, really great.'

'Is that all? Usually you are much more graphic,' said Rupert.

He was enjoying every moment. The rest of the team were loving it too.

'What's tha' want, a bloody diagram?' said Big Jack.

'That's what we usually get,' said Rupert.

'Well, this time it's different. It's not often you meet a lady,' said Big Jack.

Arthur, the fast bowler, lurched across the room choking with laughter. The rest were busily trying not to give the game away. I wanted to tell Big Jack exactly what was happening. But I didn't. Rupert was loving it.

'Do you mean you didn't score, Big Jack?' he said.

'What's tha' talking about? Took her back to my place and gave her a reet goin' over,' he said.

'Anything else?' asked Rupert.

'What's tha' want, a lantern slide lecture?' said Big Jack.

'Just your normal account of what happened,' said Rupert.

Big Jack looked around him, I prayed for the pavilion roof to fall in, or some such catastrophe to prevent what was going to happen. I wanted to interject and tell him it was a terrible practical joke. But I didn't.

'If you don't mind, I don't want to talk about the lady,' said Big Jack.

'Why?' said Rupert.

'Well, if tha' must know, I'm in love,' said Big Jack.

Rupert never moved an inch, nor did I, but we were the only two who stayed still. The rest of the team just couldn't hold it any more. Quite literally they fell about.

It was worse on the field. Every time Big Jack did something wrong, the lads would say 'Ayup, he's in love.' Back in the dressing-room getting ready for the booze-up, Rupert said, 'Seeing her tonight, Big Jack?'

'No, I'm suppin' wi't lads toneet. Tha' knows, tha' can get too much of a good thing,' he said. No one laughed.

We went to the bar and had been there an hour when she walked in. We all looked at her and then we all looked at Big Jack. He didn't know what to do. But she did. She gazed round the room, saw our party and headed towards it. Big Jack went to meet her. 'Evening love,' he said. She went past him like he didn't exist and put her arms round Rupert. 'Hello, Darling,' she said. 'Bugger me,' said Big Jack, and left.

He never came back. He left the club and joined another but never was the same again. I didn't stay either. I couldn't stand Rupert and the humiliation he had dished out.

Some time later I bumped into Big Jack. He was fatter and boozier and halfway down the backslope, but irrepressibly optimistic of his own talents. He was still the best bowler in the country, and anyone who disputed it was a nig-nog.

'Sorry about the last time we met,' I said.

'What was that?' he asked, knowing bloody well what I was talking about.

'The girl in the bar. Rupert's girl,' I said.

'Oh, her,' he said. 'Does tha' know she was one of the best birds I ever had. Did I ever tell thi' about t'time I met her outside t'bus station cafe?'

'No, Big Jack, you never told me about that,' I said.

Some time later, ten years or more after, I was guest of honour at a dinner in the North of England and I saw her.

She wasn't with Rupert, she'd obviously married someone else. She didn't recognise me, but there was no mistaking her. She looked good, blonde and cool and obviously nicely set up – and I loathed her.

I sent for the wine waiter. I pointed her out. 'Send her a port and lemon,' I said. 'A port and lemon, sir,' he said, affecting surprise. 'Tell her Big Jack sent it,' I said. He took it over and she raised an eyebrow a millionth of an inch.

Or did she?

Funny Game, Cricket

We dipped our big toe into the new season with the practice match. It meant sweet Fanny Adams because practice matches, like trial marriages, have nothing in common with the real thing. It was a pre-season ritual, a time for renewed friendships, a chance for a booze-up and an odds-on certainty that you would wake up next morning as stiff as a starched collar, creaking like a rusty hinge.

In all the years there was only one occasion when the practice match became something else, when the difference was that between a bun fight and tea-time with the Borgias. It all started with one of those incidents which proves that cricket is the great divider of communities. For such a popular game it is amazing how many regard it still as being something played by Us and not Them.

Even more amazing was the fact that in the pit village where I lived, which bred good cricketers like other people had mice, there was still a rigid demarcation between those who played cricket and those who did not. The cricketers tended to be the churchgoers and use the top pub, the rest lived on fish and chips and stood behind the goals at Barnsley. Normally they went their separate ways and pursued a policy of live and let live.

All this changed the year that the Fixtures Secretary received a letter from the bottom boozer, challenging us to a game. We held a meeting at which we decided that because it could hardly be called a first-class fixture, the game would be designated as the practice match.

This reply was not taken kindly by the lads at the bottom boozer. They asked us to put our money where our mouths were by accepting a stake of £2 a man. This would mean a bonus of £22 to the winning team, which may not seem like much now but in those days would have purchased several whippets, a decent semi-detached, a week's holiday in Blackpool staying in a good hotel, several million Woodbines and enough ale to float the Ark Royal.

Therefore, considerable interest centred around the match, and what had started out as an amiable practice session threatened to turn into an Apache uprising. We cricketers were, I must confess, a little smug about the whole affair. Frankly, we regarded our opponents as a rabble and we'd already spent the winnings.

Our optimism seemed well founded when, on the day of the match, the opposition turned up looking like the camp followers of a defeated peasant army. Instead of cricket bags they carried crates of ale which they stacked in the dressing-room until there wasn't room for the team.

'Where's your lot going to change, then,' asked our skipper.

'Change?' said their skipper incredulously. 'Does tha' think we're going to buy cricket gear for one bloody match?' 'But tha' can't play cricket like that,' said our skipper.

'Who can't?' said the leader of the bottom boozer, resplendent in flat cap, collarless shirt, waistcoat, black trousers and pit boots. And he did. And, what's more, was by far the best dressed member of his team, challenged only by the wicket-keeper, whose one concession to tradition was to whitewash his pit boots.

We won the toss and decided to bat, our skipper pointing out rather condescendingly that if we did the game would last at least until after tea.

Our confidence was unbounded, reflected in the fact that everyone volunteered to open the innings. Our wicket was such a killer that on normal match days our openers were elected by the short straw method and led to the middle blindfolded and flanked by clergy.

As it was, things didn't turn out quite as we had expected. Perhaps it was the complete unorthodoxy of our opponents that baffled us. The mixture of long hops, donkey drops and wides seemed mouth-watering, but we were destroyed by their very innocence and our own over-confidence.

Even so, we made 110, which we reckoned was about 100 too many of our opponents. We were further heartened by their attitude to the tea interval, which they used in an attempt to beat the world beer-drinking record.

They were 26 for 7 and we were counting our winnings when the man with the whitewashed boots lurched to the wicket. His name was Sid and he was wearing one pad, no gloves and a huge and ancient crutch protector which looked like a reinforced truss and which he wore not inside but outside his trousers.

Thus encumbered, oblivious both to our mirth and the gallons of beer slurping round his innards, Sid proceeded to play one of the great innings of all time. You could argue that Alletson's was more spectacular, but none has been or will be achieved in a more original manner than Sid's.

He scored 70-odd in twenty minutes without once hitting the ball with the middle of the bat. Among his more extraordinary shots was a six off the bat handle as he protected his face from a bouncer, and another six which went over the stumper's head and was achieved by Sid thwacking the ball as it passed him with the back of the bat.

He made the winning runs in inimitable style, glancing a fast full toss of his reinforced truss with a pelvic thrust which left third man standing. He was carried from the field in triumph and we were humiliated.

We sat in the dressing-room listening to the drunken rejoicing. Our skipper peeled off his socks, contemplated his feet and said 'It's a bloody funny game, is cricket,' and we nodded in agreement.

It normally took us half a season to find that out, but now we had it in the practice game before the season had even started. Nowadays I take practice matches seriously. In cricket it pays not to take anything for granted.

Cautionary Tale

The time when loyalties are laid on the line, when the wheat is sorted from the chaff, the men from the boys is during that period in our sporting calendar when the seasons overlap, when the cricket season goes into labour and we prepare to shovel muck on soccer's coffin.

It is a testing time for all sportsmen who love both games: should they watch the Cup Final like 99.9 per cent of their fellow men or should they play for their local cricket team knowing full well that it will rain all day and the cold will chill their fingers to the colour of asparagus tips.

When I was a lad there was no choice, partly because we had our priorities right, soccer being regarded as a mere interlude between cricket seasons, but mainly because our cricket started so soon after Christmas that by the time Cup Final day came around we were halfway through our fixtures. Those were splendid days when cricket really was the King and soccer was played by men who trained in billiard halls, wore their hair as short as a badger's and were about as glamorous as a team of clog dancers.

In those days – and it wasn't that long ago – there wasn't a single soccer player with the charisma of Compton or Miller, nor a football match in the whole calendar that for real sporting social, historical and sociological significance could compete with Yorkshire versus Lancashire at Bramall Lane or England v Australia at Lord's.

For all that, however, it would be wrong to assume that the overlap of the season passed us by with ne'er a ripple. We had our fair share of trouble as I shall relate. While it was generally true that the majority of us lived for cricket and came to her whenever she beckoned, there were one or two who didn't find it so easy. There were the players who excelled at both soccer and cricket and, what is more to the point, were paid for their talents. The rewards were not massive, indeed the fees covered little more than expenses and a good booze-up, but they were significant as a measure of talent – only the best got paid. What is more it was one thing to expect a soccer player to leave his club at the start of a cricket season, but quite another story if that player was on fifteen bob for soccer and cricket could only offer him ten bob and a ride to the game in a coal lorry. Which is how Pongo Blewitt came to a sticky end.

He was our opening bowler and also star performer for the local soccer team. He was christened Pongo by a soccer-mad father who wanted to commemorate the fact that Pongo Waring once played for Barnsley. Giving his son the great man's christian name was a cheaper way of doing it than erecting a statue outside the town hall.

Every season there came a time when Pongo Blewitt's talents were demanded twice over and every season save one we managed to arrange things so that he played both sports to the exclusion of neither. It worked well until the year that Pongo's football team got into the Cup Final. They played the game about five miles from where, that same day, we were playing a home fixture at cricket. We had bribed the coach driver with the soccer team to drive straight to our cricket ground after the game. The plan went wrong from the start. Pongo was late getting out of the pit so he turned up for the coach still in his pit muck. He took the field for the final looking like Pele and had a hard time against a centre-half who kept enquiring which tree he lived in. At the end of the game which they lost he ran eagerly for the bus still in his soccer gear and pit muck only to discover that the driver, in anticipation of a victory, was suffering from mild alcoholic poisoning.

Determined to the end Pongo started hitch-hiking to the cricket ground whereupon he was spotted by a housewife peering through her curtains who reported to the police that she had seen a Zulu dressed in a striped shirt and shorts thumbing a lift on the Barnsley road. It was then that Pongo had his one piece of luck because the driver of the police car was a cousin of our stumper and Pongo arrived at the cricket ground with lights flashing and tyres squealing. We were having tea.

'It's Prince Monolulu,' said our skipper, who was a schoolmaster and a bit of an intellectual.

'More like Black Beauty,' said Pongo's brother-in-law.

'Did tha' bring me cricket gear?' Pongo asked him.

'No I forgot,' said brother-in-law, who was a bit dozy.

'Well tha'r a reight pillock,' said Pongo.

'It doesn't matter,' said our skipper. He explained that Pongo's bowling talents were not needed because the other side had batted first and had been dismissed for under 100.

'It's not likely that we shall need your customary 50 today,' said the skipper sarcastically to Pongo, who had a batting average of .003. So Pongo sat in his pit muck and soccer gear and pondered the ways of the world while we went on with what we regarded as the formality of winning the game.

As it was we batted like a team of Jessies and still needed 20 to win when Pongo, our last man, went to the wicket. To say he looked incongruous is to understate the effect a man has when he walks on to a cricket field wearing a red and white striped shirt, black shorts, cricket pads and a coating of coal dust over the exposed parts of his body.

'Ayup it's Gunga Din,' said their skipper.

'Ignore them. Keep your head down and leave it to me,' said our skipper, who saw himself winning the game single-handed. Pongo took his guard. 'Could I have leg and middle please,' he asked.

'Tha'd do better wi' soap and water,' said the umpire.

Pongo could stand no more. 'Does tha' think I'm standing here looking like this because I want to, yer great twerp?' he said.

'No lip, lad,' said the umpire.

'Gollocks,' said Pongo, without moving his lips. He didn't fool the umpire.

'Tha's sent off,' he said, pointing to the pavilion.

'What for?' asked Pongo.

'Ungentlemanly conduct,' said the umpire.

'That being the case, I've something to tell thee,' said Pongo, who then cursed for ten minutes without repetition or pause for breath. He said he felt better for it and later we managed a jovial face as we sat in the boozer contemplating our extraordinary defeat. 'The Gods were against you,' said our skipper.

'Well, nowt else can happen,' said Pongo. But it did. Soon after his ninth pint and third cheese sandwich he collapsed and was whisked to hospital by ambulance. The official diagnosis was food poisoning brought about by eating a dodgy pickled onion. In fact we knew he was suffering from a sportsman's complaint called overlapping seasons.

As a postscript to this cautionary tale we could do worse than to take a tip from our drinking friends. Experienced boozers never mix the grape and the grain. It is a golden rule. Similarly, sportsmen should never make a cocktail of the seasons.

'"Gollocks," said Pongo, without moving his lips.'

Fire and Brimstone

Fast bowlers are set apart from their fellow men by a mixture of fear, envy, grudging respect and slack-mouthed admiration. In the whole of sport only the heavyweight champion of the world commands the same clutch of reactions. They carry with them on the field of play the threat of sudden violence. They are the men who probe the taproots of technique, lay bare the nerve ending. As Maurice Leyland once observed (and we must never tire of quoting the classics): 'None of us like 'em, but not all of us lets on.'

Being the son of a fast bowler I know more than a little about them. If I grew up nervous of the quickies it was only because I lived with one for a considerable length of time and although, contrary to common rumour, my old man did not eat raw meat, he undoubtedly meant business when he had a cricket ball in his hand.

Like all fast bowlers, he didn't mind whom he hit or where he hit them. Any fast bowler, if he is honest, will admit to the same attitude, and if he says different he is probably changing sex and will likely end up playing in frilly drawers with Rachel Heyhoe Flint as his captain. I am not saying that it is necessary for a fast bowler to be a homicidal maniac, but it certainly helps.

My old man was the gentlest of souls off the field, but when striding in to rocket the ball at his opponent he didn't really care whether he knocked over the batsman or the wickets.

He wasn't exactly popular in certain neighbouring villages where he left a trail of sore limbs and bruised reputations. Nor was he immune from counter-attack. As a child I remember the crowd cheering as father was carried off after being felled by the local fast bowler who repaid a broken rib from a previous encounter by hitting my old man straight between the eyes.

For a week or so thereafter he sported the most spectacular pair of black eyes outside the Panda House at London Zoo. It didn't seem to bother him too much. 'I'll bet you yon fast bowler doesn't turn up at our ground,' was all he said. And he was right, the excuse being that the fast bowler's Uncle Willy had taken a turn for the worse and needed looking after.

The presence of a really fast bowler in a team has always guaranteed a selection problem for the other side. Many's the captain who has been told on the eve of a game that one or more of his batsmen have poorly grannies or upset stomachs. Speaking personally I don't think I have ever run away from an encounter with a quick bowler, but it is also undeniably true that all my best and bravest innings against genuine pace have been played in the club bar.

I was lucky in that all the years I have played cricket, no matter what the level or the state of the track, I have never been injured, which probably argues much for my technique against pace consisting as it does of playing from a position somewhat adjacent to the square leg umpire.

Even that technique is not infallible because although it has served me well it did not prevent one of my former opening partners getting hit on every square inch of his person. He was the most accident-prone cricketer I have ever seen.

I cannot remember one game in the three seasons I played with him when he did not suffer some disaster. And if he didn't sustain an injury in the middle he would compensate by falling off his bike going home. His injuries were so frequent and varied that the local St John's Ambulance Brigade instructor used to pick him up every Monday and take him down to the village hall to let his students practice on him.

He was known as 'W. C.' because of the amount of time he spent in that establishment prior to facing a quick bowler. I used to have to knock on the door to tell him it was time to go to the middle whereupon he would emerge wan and trembling to face his weekly encounter with disaster.

He wore more protection than a medieval knight and was the only player I knew who wore two groin protectors – one a lightweight batsman's job and the other a monstrous stumper's affair which covered every part of his lower abdomen.

I was present the day he was struck in that most protected part of his body by a fast bowler of immense pace. As he lay on the floor he indicated in somewhat robust terms that the blow had trapped a certain part of his anatomy between the two boxes. The bowler took the news phlegmatically enough: 'Looks like a job for t'fire brigade then,' he said.

The thought of being attended by two fire officers wearing brass helmets and wielding oxyacetylene equipment proved too much for W. C., who retired to his favourite room in the pavilion in order to supervise his own emergency operations. I often wonder what went on at the local ambulance class the following Monday.

'he would emerge wan and trembling'

Fast bowlers make things happen because they deal in fire and spectacle. They are the flamboyant swank-pots of cricket because they carry the ultimate deterrent. Often this sense of power sends them queer in the head. For instance I knew one black quickie of fearsome pace and reputation who earned a living as a bus driver and became so convinced of his reputation as the local superman that he would not stop to pick up passengers if there was a white man at the bus stop. Thus he would often tour the town all day without stopping, his clippie snoozing contentedly on the top deck.

But generally we should forgive fast bowlers anything for they are to cricket what comets are to the heavens. Batsmen are more durable, slow bowlers have a duller and more lasting gleam, but the real speed merchants are here and gone leaving a brilliant memory trailed by a gasp of wonder.

Lillee, Thomson, Roberts, and Holding of the moderns similarly light up the present scene. On and off the field they are the centre of all attention, provoking that mixture of hostility and respect so peculiar to their breed. They handle the situation well because the fastest bowler in the world, like the best fighter, doesn't have to prove a thing in a street brawl.

I remember standing in a bar with Fred Trueman when a man shoved a tatty piece of paper under his nose, 'twixt pint and lips and said, rudely, 'Sign that.' Fred lowered his pint, slowly looked the man up and down. The man got the message. 'Would you mind very much signing your autograph, please, Mr Trueman,' he said. Fred did so without saying a word.

Once, I tried the same tactic. Coming off the field from a charity game a youth roughly grabbed my arm and stuck an autograph book under my nose. 'Put yer name on it,' he commanded. I gave him Fred's look. 'Blimey,' he said, 'Yer look like my bleedin' probation officer.'

Standing room only for the longest running show in town

Is Michael Holding's long run-up really necessary? That was the question posed recently by Mr Jack Fingleton, who argued that it wasn't, and that it slowed the rhythm of a game to the point where you could barely feel its heartbeat. I agree. What is more, I am something of an expert in these matters, having once played cricket with a fast bowler whose run was so long that it makes Holding's five-minute walk back to his mark look positively economic.

He played in the village team in which I served my cricketing apprenticeship, and was one of the most extraordinary sporting eccentrics I have ever met. He was tall and thin as a nail; indeed, I have seen more meat on a glass eye. His life's frustration was that he wanted to be a fast bowler more than anything else, but the Great Umpire had given him the physique of a famine victim.

He compensated for his physical frailty by using every available contraption to strengthen his body. He wound crêpe bandages around his ankles, wore elastic knee supports and climaxed his dressing-room ritual by climbing into an abdominal truss. Thus attired, he looked like someone the St John Ambulance Brigade had been practising on. His boots were even more remarkable. The most feared quick bowler in our area at that time was an old pro who wore specially-made boots with a gleaming stainless steel toe-cap on his right boot to counter his drag.

Not to be outdone, our fast bowler made his own toe-cap out of an old treacle tin, arguing that although he really didn't need it because he didn't drag his toe in the delivery stride, it was, nonetheless, a potent psychological weapon. He could not comprehend that it was unlikely that any batsman would be frightened by a bowler who had Tate and Lyle across his toe-cap.

But the most extraordinary aspect of this totally unique

cricketer was his run-up. It was so long that it did not fit our ground. The only way they could accommodate him was to cut a gap in the hedge at his favourite end, to allow him to cross the lane bounding our ground and make his mark in the barley field beyond.

It was from the far distance, thigh deep in barley, that he began his run. It would be good to report that for all its inordinate length, his progress to the wicket was a delight to the eye. Alas, as I think back over the years, I can only liken his run-up to a man dodging a sniper. He zig-zagged, ducked, bucked-and-winged for a full 30 yards before executing a weird Ali shuffle which prepared him for the second part of his journey. This consisted of a variety of leaps and bounds which carried him a further 30 yards to the crease. His first problem on reaching the crease was that he was too knackered to do anything but let the ball go at a gentle medium-pace. His second problem had to do with the extravagance of his final leap which meant, more often than not, that he was nearer the batsman than the umpire when he finally parted with the ball.

We tried everything to cure his fault, but nothing worked. For instance, our skipper, a kindly man, suggested that he might try bowling a yard or two back from the stumps. The first time our bowler experimented, he came charging out of the barley, through the gap in the hedge and then became confused to the point where he let go of the ball some 30 yards away from the batsman. The ball was impeded in its flight to the batsman by the formidable bulk of the umpire, and it struck that unfortunate soul on the back of the head, dropping him like a sack of potatoes.

Our bowler was, moreover, an acute embarrassment when playing away from home on grounds which did not allow for his exceedingly long run. We played at one place which did have a gate for him to run through, but unfortunately was skirted by a busy main road. When he marked his run out, he started in the car park of the local boozer, and crossed the road on the first phase of his journey to the crease.

He was taken off by order of the police after a bus driver employed by the Yorkshire Traction Bus Company reported a near miss on a journey to Barnsley when, on a clear road and in good visibility, he executed a sudden emergency stop due to the appearance of a man wearing a white suit who had shot out of the pub car park and pranced across the road in front of him, before disappearing through a gate into the cricket field opposite. Similar sightings by motorists out for a weekend drive in various parts of South Yorkshire were too numerous to ignore, and forced our bowler to the crisis point of his life.

This, inevitably, required him to change his run. But he refused to cut down its length, choosing instead to incorporate all of it in a curve which didn't require him to depart the ground, but which meant that his approach to the wicket started at the square-leg umpire. Thus he ran a huge U, the first 30 yards, directly towards the barley field before swinging round to double back on himself as he approached the wicket. He only played a couple of seasons. He didn't have the stamina. He tried adding extra support bandages to his spindly limbs, but he couldn't overcome the severe handicap imposed on his ambitions by his miserable physique and total lack of talent.

One day the tin fell off his toe-cap. That was the end. He sat in the pavilion, toe-cap in hand, looking crestfallen.

'What's up?' asked our skipper.

'Shall I get a new toe-cap?' said the bowler.

'If tha' likes,' said the skipper without enthusiasm. 'And while you're at it, why doesn't tha' get a steel plate for thi' head.'

Our bowler got the message and retired. I never saw the likes of his run-up again until I saw Michael Holding's. There the similarity ends. I would not mind facing our fast bowler even now, whereas I could only be persuaded to face Mr Holding following a large cash transaction, and providing he was made to wear deep-sea diver's boots and lead weights round his middle. And even then I would insist that the ball had a bell in it.

Yon Laads are Reet Cobbers

In an ever changing world there are but two tribes remaining with the traditional view that life is centred round strong beer, docile women and good cricket – not necessarily in that order. They are called Australians and Yorkshiremen. It is my firm conviction that, when Britain severed relations with its colonies and joined the Common Market in the mistaken belief that we could find anything in common with wogs who don't play cricket, Yorkshire should immediately have declared UDI, appointed Fred Trueman Prime Minister and signed a Treaty of Alignment with Australia.

When I was a kid I was brought up to respect and hate the Australians. I was told that they would rob, cheat and go to any lengths to win at cricket. 'Just like us' said my old man, 'us' meaning Yorkshire and not England. My lasting memories of cricket in my childhood are to do with being taken by my father to see the Australians at Bramall Lane or Headingley. There was then, as there is now, a special look about an Australian and a Yorkshire side as it takes the field. Others look rag, tag and bobtail as they come down the pavilion steps, but the Aussies and the Tykes, no matter whether they are a great side or a poor one, always resemble a powerful and intimidating body of men.

The first time I saw the Australians was just after the war and we went to Bramall Lane, rising with the birds so that we could get there three hours before start of play to ensure admittance. Even then we had to sit on the grass. If memory serves me, Hutton and Lowson opened for Yorkshire and certainly it was Lindwall who bowled the first over for Australia. His first ball was wide down the leg side and went into the crowd for four byes. The fielder at fine leg waited for the ball to come out of the crowd and became increasingly restive when it didn't appear. Finally it was handed to him, whereupon he started laughing and called over the umpire.

The ball, shining red and new only minutes before, was now as dirty and scuffed as a small boy's toe-cap. Some Yorkshireman sitting in the crowd had rubbed it in the dirt and removed all vestige of shine. A new ball was ordered. 'Silly bugger,' said my old man. 'He ought to have just rubbed a bit off so they didn't notice.'

That day I couldn't take my eyes off Lindwall. It was my first look at a great fast bowler and from that day on, whenever he played in the county, I went to see him. Once I cycled the thirty miles to Bradford to see him bowl at Hutton. I would have walked twice that distance if needs be to see the connoisseur's delight, the master bowler attacking the complete batsman.

Yorkshire batted and I shall never forget the Australians taking the field with fifteen thousand pairs of Yorkshire eyes on Lindwall as he went through his limbering-up routine, every man in the crowd wishing he'd do himself a serious injury. Then the roar as Hutton came to the wicket, pale faced under the blue cap, the man whose wicket the Australians prized the most, the player to whom Lindwall paid the supreme compliment of never bowling badly to him.

Hutton took guard and complete silence fell upon the ground. I swear that, as Lindwall began his approach to the wicket, one of cricket's most menacing and thrilling sights, you could hear his footsteps on the turf. He bowled the perfect ball, an inswinging yorker, and Hutton's stumps rocked in their sockets like drunken sailors. The Australians rejoiced like only they can and the Yorkshire crowd reacted to bitter, numbing disappointment with an uncanny stillness. Crestfallen, Hutton walked back to the pavilion and the crowd was so hushed you could hear him take his gloves off.

'What's tha' reckon to that then?' asked the man behind me to his neighbour as Hutton disappeared into the pavilion. 'Not much,' said his friend. 'But I'll tell thi' what, I wish that buggar Lindwall had been born in Leeds.' Raymond Russell Lindwall, for all he is assured of his place among the immortals of cricket, never knew higher praise than that.

Any comparison of cricketing stories, apocryphal or otherwise, about Australian and Yorkshire cricketers, underlines the similarities between the two tribes. By which I mean that a story summing up the Yorkshireman's attitude to the game would be equally accurate and authentic-sounding if copied word for word with 'Australian' substituted for 'Yorkshire'.

It is no matter of chance that one of the best stories on cricket was written by an Australian about playing in Yorkshire. I am referring to Jack Fingleton's magnificent account of playing at Bramall Lane with Bradman's team in 1938 when Yorkshire came within an inch of winning. What sets the piece apart from others is Fingleton's perception of the affinities between the two teams, the matching of a supreme pair of gamecocks.

He summed it up precisely with this passage about the team's arrival at Bramall Lane:

It is easy to mistake the atmosphere that receives rather than greets you on this ground. It seems to bristle with belligerence. The looks bore through you in cold analysis as you go to the nets before the game. At Lord's, going to the nets, one is greeted with cheery nods and smiles and often a call of 'good luck'. There's none of that at Bramall Lane. . . . The grim look of the spectators, the postures and the gestures of the eleven robust Yorkshiremen with the white rose on their caps all issue a challenge to the Australians and it runs something like this: 'We are Yorkshire. Tha's playin' wi' cricket fire laad when tha' cooms here. We're noo abaht to show tha' laad, tha's noot sa good as tha' thinks.'

One can argue with the accent but not with the article's real authenticity of mood and attitude.

It was at Bramall Lane, alas a cricket ground no more, that I saw the final starburst from the sublime player and entertainer Fred Trueman. Like the actor he was, Fred chose the setting and the occasion carefully. Bramall Lane was where he started as a young, raw tearaway and it was on the same ground twenty seasons later in 1968 that he gave us the last look of a great fast bowler and old sweat in action.

He skippered the Yorkshire side that day and, after winning the toss and contributing a typically swashbuckling and humorous innings, declared at 355 for nine. He opened the bowling himself off his long run and for the last time we were privileged to see this man being what he always claimed he was, 't'best fast bowler that ever drew breath'.

In this, his last match at Bramall Lane, he showed the entire repertoire of his talents, not just his bowling and his batting but his fielding too, reminding us that he was one of the best close fielders in the world when he dived far to his right at second slip to catch Doug Walters off Richard Hutton.

Directed by Trueman, who ran the entire operation with the panache of a theatrical impresario, Yorkshire beat the Australians by an innings and sixty runs, the first time they had beaten the tourists since 1902. It was Trueman's swansong and it was fitting he should have achieved it against a team he regarded as the dearest of enemies.

One story sums up completely Fred Trueman's attitude towards the Australians. It was on his last tour down under and Fred was becoming increasingly impatient with being told that everything in Australia was newer and superior in comparison to anything else. This, he reckoned, was the prerogative of the Yorkshireman and not the upstart Aussie. His patience broke when he was shown the Sydney Harbour Bridge.

'What do you think of our bridge?' asked his host as they surveyed the majestic structure. 'Your bridge? *Our* bloody bridge, you should say. Buggar me, a Yorkshire firm, Dorman & Long, built it . . . and you bastards still haven't paid for it.'

Away from Home

Like women who kiss and run, sporting tours promise much but give nothing. It is as true of the international tour as it is of the local club tour. The only thing our footballers learned when they ventured to Mexico was how to do the Aztec Two-step to combat Montezuma's Revenge. Similarly, our lads in the West Indies become adept at the Trinidadian Turkey-trot in avoidance of the Caribbean Cruise.

The local club tour is similarly fraught. To start with, the basic premise of these tours is a damnable lie. Club members talk themselves into believing that they are going on tour to play cricket or rugby or whatever against some good opposition. In fact a group of men are running away from wives and girlfriends to get drunk and, if possible, have a bit of skirt in a hayfield.

Drink is the serious problem, particularly on cricket tours, for it can be said without fear of contradiction that nothing yet devised by man is worse for a sick hangover than a day's cricket in the summer sun. The morning after the night before the most you can pray for is to win the toss and bat and hope to God that your openers will bat all day.

When we had to field first anything could happen, and sometimes did. I once saw our fast bowler, drunk as a squaddie at eleven in the morning, race in to deliver the first ball of the day, flatten the umpire at his end, crash through the wickets and deliver a beamer from ten yards down the pitch which all but decapitated the umpire at square leg. Moreover, he had the temerity to appeal, although we never did discover what for, nor whom he expected to judge his appeal, as both adjudicators were stretched flat on the turf.

He was led from the pitch, moaning gently, to be followed shortly by our wicket-keeper, who sat down during a drinks break and fell into a drunken slumber from which he refused to be roused.

On that same tour the stumper became involved in an incident that changed his whole life. We were touring Derbyshire,

89

and we were having a farewell drink at Buxton before moving on to Matlock the next day. Our wicket-keeper, an argumentative drunk, became involved in a dispute with our scorer about who had the best sense of direction.

This somewhat aimless argument took on an altogether more meaningful aspect when the scorer bet the stumper he couldn't find his way at night on foot from Buxton to Matlock. The stumper accepted, and thus it was that one midsummer night, with the stars glinting, he set off with many a drunken farewell. His money had been taken from him to prevent his cheating by taking a taxi.

The next day we arrived in our bus at Matlock, and our stumper hadn't turned up. Later on we phoned the law because we were worried about him. Three weeks later we had a letter from him postmarked Buenos Aires, saying that he had met this dusky beauty and intended to marry her, and would we send him his money because he'd need a few bob for the wedding.

Another problem with tours is that, on the whole, the opposition is likely to be the kind that can't get fixtures with neighbouring clubs, which is why many of our opponents on tour were the inmates of various institutions, both penal and mental. It was while playing at one of the latter that I came across two of the most extraordinary sporting characters I have ever met.

The first was an opening bat who wore only a single pad as he had one tin leg. He had a remarkable style which centred around his ability to strike the ball to all parts of the field, sometimes with his bat, but more often with his tin leg. This, of course, was in the days before the change of rule about leg-byes, and often he would score a quick thirty with all but ten coming from his leg.

Appealing for LBW was a waste of time because the two local umpires, both inmates of the same institution as the batsman, regarded it as a huge joke. For instance, in the first over, our opening bowler had a good delivery kicked off middle stump for four byes. The ball hitting the leg made a sound like a bell. He appealed loudly to the umpire, who thought for a moment and said, 'One o'clock and all's well.'

The same team had a fast bowler who wore a monocle and ran to the wicket with a ball in either hand. He was completely ambidextrous, so that batsman had no idea from which hand the ball was coming. His speciality was to bowl with both arms simultaneously, and he had an even subtler variation whereby he would deliver one ball off the wrong foot, followed a moment later by another delivery from a normal action.

Any batsman who exercised his right to inquire of the umpire what kind of delivery to expect was given the totally disarming answer. 'I'm blowed if I know.'

Anyone who has ever been on a sporting tour will know I am speaking the truth when I say that when it comes to playing away from home, sport imitates life in that we would be better off if we stayed in our own back yard.

'often he would score a quick thirty with all but ten coming from his leg'

This Sporting North

What the northerner has never swallowed is that old lie about the game being the thing. He differs from his counterpart in the south by his ardent belief that sport is about winning and all the better if played for money.

A look at the very grass roots of northern sporting society sums up the attitude and spells out the difference. The northern lad who shows any talent for cricket will have his skill tested by competitive league cricket from the moment he leaves the cradle. If he's any good at the game he will turn professional playing for a few quid a match. The southern habit of playing friendly matches for love is not understood in the north, where 'friendly' is the last word to describe any game whether it be soccer or cribbage. Similarly, those enlightened gentlemen who run Rugby Union from Twickenham woo the twin corpses of non-competitive rugby and amateurism while their northern brothers who have no time for such conceits have made a better game for themselves and the people who watch it.

From the very start of his life the northern child is taught to feel sport with the nerve ends. The proper appreciation of a game is passed down from father to son like a family heirloom. It is summed up in that famous story of the young lad who arrived breathless at a cricket ground in Yorkshire to find his father in rapt contemplation of the game. 'Dad, dad, I've got terrible news. Our kid's got diphtheria, police are after me grandad, mother's run off wi' t'milkman and t'house has burned down,' he said. Father turned to son with real sorrow in his eyes and said: 'Ay, and I've got worse news for thee . . . Hutton's out.'

It is perhaps in this anguished voice from the terraces that we come nearest to understanding northern attitudes to sport. It ranges from the choral wit of the Liverpool Kop to the individual solos of despair that can be heard on any soccer or cricket ground, in the north. One Lancashire league cricket team had a supporter of such original wit and style that he became as big an attraction as the star players. His name was

Alwyn Nightingale, and his sayings are remembered in the leagues as well as any innings by Constantine or Everton Weekes.

One of the best Nightingale stories concerns a local 'derby' game with his team playing away from home. The opposition had lately acquired a spanking new motor-roller, and with inordinate pride this was driven round the ground to loud applause before the start of the game. All went well until the machine came opposite Alwyn.

'What the bloody hell's that,' he bellowed at the groundsman.

The groundsman stopped the machine and faced his tormentor. 'It's a brand new motor-roller, that's what it is,' he said with real pride.

'That's nowt to brag abart. We've got a donkey to pull t'roller at our place,' said Alwyn.

'What's so special abart that then?' shouted the groundsman.

'It's got gold bloody teeth, that's what,' said Alwyn.

It might have been Alwyn Nightingale who after forty years of watching soccer finally managed a ticket for the Cup Final by winning one in a raffle. He arrived at Wembley early and as time for kick-off drew nigh was horrified to see two vacant seats next to him. With five minutes to go one of the seats was taken by another north countryman, who was immediately engaged in conversation by his neighbour.

'What's tha' reckon then. I've been following soccer for forty years and have never managed a Cup Final ticket, then I win one in a raffle and come to Wembley and what do I find? Only that there's a spare seat next to me. I call it disgusting, what's tha' reckon?'

The newly arrived man looked at him with understanding. 'I agree old lad, but tha' sees unfortunately that seat was for t'wife but sadly she passed away two days ago.'

The first man was only slightly miffed by this. 'Well I'm reet sorry to hear that but none the less surely tha' should have got rid of thi' ticket. Surely tha' could have given it to some of thi' relatives or neighbours,' he said.

'Oh, I tried right enough, I tried both family and friends but they're a reet miserable lot. Not a sportsman among 'em. They all went to t'bloody funeral instead.'

Apocryphal? Certainly, but only someone who did not comprehend the northerner's passionate involvement in sport would call it far-fetched. The fact is that the northerner twigged a long time ago that sport was an important and necessary part of his life. It is more than an entertainment, it engages the very soul of a man stretching his emotions to their limits. I see nothing eccentric in this devotion to sport, the eccentricity is in someone who cannot understand that watching Manchester United year in and year out is as important to some men as going to Glyndebourne is to others.

Not only important but as rewarding in every sense. This passion among northern spectators is echoed by their heroes on the field of play. It is no fluke that Yorkshire has for so long dominated county cricket in this country, nor is it by chance that northern soccer teams like Manchester United, Newcastle, Everton, Liverpool and Leeds United have taken most of the honours since the war. Why? Well Manchester City's ex-manager, Malcolm Allison, himself a southerner, is in no doubt. He said that southern teams are 'too soft'.

Similarly, the Yorkshire cricket team has suffered the same false reputation among people who might be envious of their stupendous success but who more likely, having been reared on southern cricket, wouldn't know anything about the game in any case. All the attitudes of northerners to sport, wherever they might live and whatever the sport, are embodied in the way that Yorkshire plays its cricket. There is the fierce partisan pride which reveals itself in the fact that to play for Yorkshire you must be born in the county; there is the bloody-mindedness which produces characters like Trueman and Johnny Wardle, and there is the belief that games are meant to be won, as revealed in Yorkshire's astonishing record of championship wins.

What you will see when Yorkshire play, is eleven men working together towards doing the other man down and not minding how they do it. It is the same attitude that makes Leeds United the team it is, that lifts Harvey Smith out of the ordinary, that brings the best and the worst out of the Stretford Enders when Manchester United take the field. It's to do with the clay that shaped them, the air they breathe and what's bred in the bone. It doesn't do to enquire further.

Cody's Congs

I suppose that when they come to write the history of football, one of the most significant events of the present era will be seen to be the emergence of the manager out of the shadows and into the spotlight. In the murky past, though, there were always exceptions; the manager was the man who paid the wages, made sure the balls were blown up and weeded the terracing. It was not a glamorous job and, in the main, it begat anonymity, although there was one manager who achieved both fame and glamour, albeit in an unusual way.

He became enamoured of the tea lady at the club, and they spent many magic moments together when he should have been weeding the terracing, and she should have been making the tea.

The scene of their romantic interludes was the directors' toilet, it being the perfect secret meeting place for lovers because it was uninhabited except on match days. One day the passionate couple managed to lock themselves in, and had to be rescued by the fire brigade. No one believed the manager's excuse that he was looking for his cufflinks, and that the tea lady had been helping him. The matter was discreetly reported in the local paper, and there were an extra 2000 at the next home game hoping to catch a glimpse of the tea lady.

Little did we know at the time that there would come a day when managers like Clough and Allison would pull in the crowds without having to indulge in such bizarre escapades. Mind you, it's my view that managers have always been slightly potty. We notice them more nowadays because what happens on the field is infinitely less interesting than that which happens in the manager's office.

The best manager I ever played for bossed a team called Cody's Congs. He was manager and one-man board of directors because he owned the field, the footballs, the nets and the lorry which took us to away games.

He also owned the shirts which gave us our name. What happened was that he had a brother-in-law who worked for

Cody's Circus which went bust. Our manager bought a lot of
the bankrupt stock, including a dozen T-shirts which differed
from ordinary football shirts only in that they had names and
not numbers on the backs. Thus I became the only centre-
forward that I know of to play a season with Ramon The Dwarf
on my back.

The tactical advantages of our strip were enormous. Not
many defenders looking for our right-winger tumbled he was
Carlos the Fire Eater, or that our inside-right was the man
with Sheba and Her Pythons on his back. We took full advantage of their bewilderment and went through a season
undefeated. Sadly for us and the cause of brighter football, we
were ordered by the league's management committee to wear
traditional shirts for the coming seasons.

This precipitated a financial crisis in the club which was
solved by Elsie, our manager's wife. During the summer she
knitted an entire set of football shirts. So it came to be that we
took the field for the opening game of the season attired in
shirts of double-strength fisherman's yarn which would have
been useful for arctic explorers but were entirely unsuitable for
ninety minutes non-stop action on a soccer pitch. We only
wore them once because the first time Elsie washed them they

shrunk, so we were back to the Cody's Circus shirts, which we wore inside out to hide the name tags.

Elsie was a great one with the knitting needles. She once knitted a pullover for a chicken in our team colours. Our manager kept chickens, and one day after selecting a bird for the pot and wringing its neck, was half-way through plucking it when the unfortunate bird revived. Our manager didn't have the heart to finish the job off, so he settled for a bird with a sore neck and minus half its feathers. It became our mascot and the ever-practical Elsie knitted it a little jumper to keep it warm.

Sadly, the wretched creature didn't last long because one of our manager's neighbours with a cruel sense of humour complained that the bird was upsetting his wife, who had seen it leaving the outside toilet buttoning its flies. Whereas the rest of us appreciated the joke, our manager and Elsie took it seriously and our mascot ended up on the dinner table with a pound of sage and onion stuffed inside it.

Elsie was the mother figure to our football team. She washed the kit, made the tea, patched our wounds, darned our socks and, for a time, became the only woman trainer in the whole of football. This experiment lasted only until Bill Clacker, our centre-half, got kicked in the unmentionables and was altogether too precise in his language when Elsie arrived on the scene and asked him what had happened.

Her only other venture on to the field of play was during a particularly dirty game against a local pit team, when the opposing centre-forward put our goalkeeper and the ball in the back of the net. Herbert, our goalkeeper, belonged to Elsie. I say belonged, because although he called her Mam, he wasn't her son. Rumour was that Elsie had a sister in Barnsley who had an affair with an Italian prisoner of war and Herbert was the issue of that unlikely liaison. However, no Mum could have loved a son as passionately as Elsie loved Herbert.

The sight of him lying bloodied in the back of the net was too much. As the centre-forward turned to embrace his colleagues, he was confronted by Elsie, who bashed him with her handbag. She would have done worse, had she not been grabbed by the referee.

Thereafter she stayed at home, which proved a wise decision, because during the return game the centre-forward she had assaulted brought along his mother, who looked a bit like Sydney Greenstreet, except she weighed more.

'What happened to thi' mother?' asked the centre-forward. 'Got knocked down by a bus,' lied Herbert.

'That's nowt to what's going to happen to thee,' said the centre-forward. And he was as good as his word.

Among her many talents, Elsie was a soothsayer. Every Saturday morning at the team gathering she would empty the cups and read the tea leaves. Our right-winger, Charlie Donkin, wouldn't play if the message wasn't favourable.

'You will meet a big black man today,' Elsie would say, peering at the tea leaves.

'Blackies don't play football,' said Charlie.

'He's in his pit muck,' Elsie explained.

'Owt else?' asked Charlie.

'A white man and a man in a white coat,' said Elsie.

'Christ, an ambulance,' said Charlie. 'I'm going to get a leg broke.'

'Load of nonsense,' said our manager.

But it made no difference. Charlie went home and stayed in bed, only getting up at opening time to go to the boozer, whereupon he was knocked down by an ice-cream van driven by a man wearing a white overall. He didn't break his leg, but it cured him of Elsie.

I digress only to underline the problem facing the manager of a football team, whether it be Cody's Congs or Leeds United. Our manager stuck with Cody's Congs for about four seasons until he discovered the joys of women's football. He organised a team from the local stocking factory, and ended up leaving Elsie and her knitting needles to live in sin with his centre-half, a strapping lass with legs like Bobby Charlton.

Now all that happened a long time ago, but surely the peccadilloes of our present race of football managers only go to show that nothing has changed. Managers of football teams are the odd bods of our society. The axiom that you have to have a slate loose to be a football manager is as true today as it ever was. I'm not saying you have to be barmy to manage a football team, but it certainly helps.

Facts of Life

The idea that sport and sex do not mix is firmly implanted in British thinking. We further believe that sport is the antidote to sex, that evil thoughts about girlies are banished by a brisk game of table tennis, followed by a cold shower. It is my theory that we achieved our reputation as a nation of sports lovers not because we are particularly fond of sport but because we are appallingly shy about sex.

In other words, the playing fields of England are full of young people, not because their parents are desperately keen for them to learn the skills of football, but because they hope to delay the awful day when their boy discovers that girls are deliciously different from himself.

We have clung to this belief when all the evidence points in the opposite direction and only serves to show that the playing fields of England are training grounds for the bed chamber. Women adore sportsmen and any youth who is packed off by his parents in search of healthy and innocent sport on the playing field is, in truth, being launched on a collision course towards members of the opposite sex.

But before they do I have a cautionary tale to tell involving sex and Squat White. Squat was the inside-right in a team I used to play with, a good footballer but strikingly unbeautiful. He was in fact the first captain of my first World Ugly XI. The team we played for was called the Congs, an abbreviation of the Congregational Chapel. None of us actually attended the Chapel, except our captain, who ran the team in the fond belief that football was spiritually uplifting and that we should all benefit by kicking lumps off one another every Saturday afternoon.

He received his first lesson in disenchantment the day we played a cup game at a nearby pit village. Our opponents included five brothers who formed a defence which kept the local outpatients department in regular employment. We were changing under a railway bridge near the ground (which made a pleasant change from stripping in the hedge bottom as was normal) when the five brothers appeared.

'Which one is it, then?' asked the biggest one.

'I beg your pardon,' said our captain.

'Which one of your lot got our Gladys in trouble, then?' asked another brother.

Our captain went pale with rage. How dare these monsters suggest that one of his team would dally with their Gladys. Didn't they know that football kept a young man free from such evil thoughts. He had just started saying as much when the biggest brother interrupted.

'Don't deny it. Tha's only got to look at our Gladys to see what happened. She's in trouble and she says that it wor a Cong that did it. She won't gi' us his name but we're going to find out and when we do then he's got a choice.'

'What's that?' said the captain.

'Church or t'Infirmary,' said the big brother, glaring at the lot of us.

They left us saying they would give us until the start of the game to name the culprit. Our skipper looked around. 'Who's been playing silly buggers, then?' he said.

Slowly Squat White raised his hand. At first we didn't believe him. He was the last person you would expect anyone called Gladys to fall for. But he finally convinced us with a graphic description of how Gladys had accosted him after one game, told him he looked like Peter Doherty and asked him to accompany her on a blackberrying expedition.

'Will I have to wed her?' said Squat.

'Does tha' want to?' asked the skipper.

Squat shook his head. 'But I don't want to end up in t'Infirmary either,' he said.

'Well, we'll just have to tell 'em that they've made a mistake, that their Glady's got mixed up in t'teams,' said the skipper.

The brothers greeted this news contemptuously. The biggest one said: 'We'll just have to clog t'lot of you to mek sure that t'culprit doesn't escape.' His brothers nodded in agreement and seemed delighted at the prospect ahead. There were times during the ensuing ninety minutes when all of us felt like squealing on Squat, if only to stop the kicking, gouging and hacking. But we battled silently on and finished losing 5–0 with six men still standing.

At the final whistle the biggest brother said: 'We'll be coming for you when we've got changed and we'll have t'old man wi' us and some of his mates to sort you lot out proper.'

We fled to our bridge, grabbed our clothes and, without bothering to change, ran fearfully to the bus-stop carrying our wounded. On the bus our skipper said to Squat, 'Tha's disappointed me, Squat. Tha' sees now wheer all this petticoat-hunting' leads thi'.'

Squat nodded miserably.

A few weeks later Gladys shopped Squat to her brothers and they came looking for him. Being a sensible lad, he decided on marriage, rather than an unspecified time in the Infirmary, and left our club to join his brothers-in-law.

The real casualty in the affair was our skipper, who was cruelly shown that far from sport being an antidote to sex that he believed it was in fact an aphrodisiac. He gave up football and bought some racing pigeons. I regarded what happened as a useful experience, one that enabled me to give sport its proper place in the rich tapestry of life.

For instance, when I bought my eldest son his first pair of football boots I knew exactly what I was doing. Not keeping him out of trouble but equipping him for the first round of the battle of the sexes.

Why Charlie Ran Away with the Ball

I once sat in the pavilion at Bramall Lane, next to a man who throughout the day kept the most meticulous chronicle of play in a vast pile of charts and scorebooks.

I asked him if this was his hobby and he told me it was more than that. He travelled home and away with Yorkshire, taking with him his charts and scoreboards. He had an attic full of them at home.

When I remarked that this seemed an unusual kind of pastime he looked at me sadly and said: 'Ah, but you don't quite understand. One day when I'm at a Yorkshire game something will happen in the scorebox, something will go wrong, and then I shall be the only person on the ground who knows what the exact state of the game is.'

So far as I know he is still touring the country with Yorkshire and still awaiting his big chance. It is such a selfless ambition that I've often felt like helping him out by kidnapping the scorers at gunpoint during the lunch interval or setting fire to the scorebox. The legal consequences would pale against the sight of my friend being borne in triumph from the pavilion by anxious officials. A lifetime's devotion such as his deserves some recognition.

At least his is a more practical fantasy than the ones possessed by most sportlovers. In the dear, distant days when I used to stand behind the goals at Barnsley my friend Herbert Brown used to turn up wearing a complete strip in Barnsley's colours underneath his normal dress. He also wore football boots and shin pads, which came in useful on more than one occasion when things got rough at our end of the ground.

His fantasy was that one day Barnsley would find themselves a man short and the team manager would make an impassioned plea for reinforcements over the loudspeaker. At this point Herbert planned to leap the barrier on to the field and walk nonchalantly towards the players' tunnel while slowly disrobing. All this he confessed to us but he kept the last half of his dream to himself. He never told a soul what he anticipated would happen once he took the field with his heroes, although anyone with any experience of these things will know that he expected to score a dramatic hat-trick, be signed on by the club at a record fee, play for England and crown a distinguished career by marrying Miss Barnsley and taking a boozer.

He waited patiently for many years for his big chance but it never came. When Barnsley took the drop into the Third Division he announced that he had given up any hopes of playing for them because he didn't want to start his career with a third division side. From that point on he devoted his attention to our local team.

His presence at our games was an acute embarrassment to us because we all knew that underneath the overcoat, pullover, waistcoat and combinations there lurked a footballer just aching to strip off and take the field. We used to give him little jobs to do to ease our conscience. First he was put in charge of the match ball. After he had accepted this appointment we started getting complaints from the players that the balls were always heavy and slippery. The mystery was solved some time later when an official of the club called on Herbert to talk the matter over and found him pegging the football on the washing line. He explained proudly that he always put the ball in with the wife's weekly wash and hung it out to dry just before the game.

We rewarded his enterprise by appointing him trainer and thereby made him the completely happy man. It was a position which allowed his fantasies full rein. He bought himself a scarlet track-suit and a large black bag for his equipment. He had little cards printed which said on them 'Herbert Brown RAMC (Retd). Cures without Pain.' He brought a new and largely invented vocabulary to his job. A simple strain became a 'severe horritosis of the right termicular', a sprained ankle was called 'a grave contusion of the starboard fetlock'. His flair and enthusiasm gave him a new standing in the community. People used to come to him with their aches and pains and before long he retired as our trainer and set up in private practice in the back room of his council house. He was the only example I know of one's sporting fantasies bringing anything other than disenchantment and grief.

I was telling this story to a friend of mine who played Rugby

League in his younger days and he recalled a similar tale of fulfilled sporting fantasy. He was playing for a club in Lancashire and every home game a character called Charlie would invade the dressing-room and ask what he might do. After a while they decided that his job should be to collect the balls that were kicked out of the ground and always make certain that there was a ball in play. Now this seemingly simple task was made difficult, not to say impossible, by the fact that the ground sloped downhill towards one goal and any kick in that direction was certain to carry out of the ground and down the hill towards the local bowling greens.

My friend, who was an expert goal kicker, reckoned that on a good day he'd have the ball out of the ground on twenty occasions. But Charlie, like all sports lovers, proved himself equal to the task.

Every time the ball whistled out of the ground he would set off at a gallop, coat flying round his head, scattering the bowlers on the greens, to retrieve the ball. Often as he was racing back with his capture another ball would come sailing out of the ground and Charlie would have to decide whether to return the ball he was carrying and then set off after the ball now passing over his head, or whether to give chase immediately and return with both footballs, in which case he could guarantee that a third would whistle over his head when he was halfway through his return journey.

It was the manner in which he faced up to these momentous decisions that won him fame and respect. His enthusiastic and colourful cursing as he went about his task gained him an audience all to himself, and as many people used to pay to see Charlie at work as came to see the game itself. At half-time he would be allowed a refreshing lemon with the players and would admonish my friend the goalkicker thus: 'I'm knackered. Can't tha' cut down on t'power, lad. I'm working harder than a seaside donkey.'

He stuck it for a few seasons and then one day when my friend was having a field day kicking goals from every angle they suddenly ran out of balls. The teams waited for Charlie but nothing happened. After the match they asked some of the bowlers what had happened and the nearest they got to an answer was that mid-way through the second half Charlie came charging across the greens in pursuit of a ball and just kept on running. They watched him to the horizon and thought it strange but didn't worry too much.

My friend didn't see Charlie again until many seasons later, when he went to watch a match in Wakefield and saw Charlie selling programmes. He didn't talk to him because he felt that it might be cruel to have Charlie relive the horror of the day when he ran away from his ambitions.

We shouldn't laugh at the Charlies and the Herbert Browns of the sporting scene. All of us who are addicted to a sport nurse our secret and foolish ambitions. Only the totally innocent or the masochists reveal them to their fellow men.

Skull Skill 1

Funny how the trapdoor of my memory is sprung by incidents of the moment. Only the other day I was minding my own business, taking a stroll, when I happened on a game of soccer. Two local teams were hard at it, boring the pants off the three spectators and each other, when there occurred something that reached into the back pocket of my mind.

One of the teams gained a free kick just outside the penalty area and it was taken by a player built like a butcher's dog and wearing the demeanour of the village hangman. He raced thirty yards and toe-ended the ball, heavy as a suet pudding, at the wall of defenders. The velocity of the shot was sufficient to cause the wall to break and scatter all except one player who not only remained at his post but flung himself headlong at the missile.

When the top of his head hit the ball the impact must have been similar to two inter-city trains colliding head-on. Surprisingly though, the defender with the kamikaze tendencies survived, nay, more than that, he prospered. The ball hurtled from his head way over the halfway line and the centre-forward, who was enjoying a break while picking his nose, nipped through to score. 'He does it regular,' said the local standing next to me. 'Can't play football but he can't half head a ball.'

I was back in time twenty years or so and standing on the terraces at Barnsley watching a centre-half called Archie Whyte, who would head cannon balls. He had the broadest brow of anyone I've ever seen, including Beethoven, and it was pock-marked and hillocked with the scars of his craft.

He was something, but the best of them all was 'Muscle' Eadie. He was a large, friendly youth with a large unfriendly mother who prepared her son for life's highways and byways by regularly thumping him on the head with a small coal shovel. Having survived a dozen or more years of this treatment he developed an immunity to blows on his skull and on

'regularly thumping him on the head with a small coal shovel'

the football field gained a considerable reputation as a header of the ball.

Although he played centre-half for our team his speciality was saving penalty kicks. Whenever we had one awarded against us, which was just about every game, Muscle would send the goalie away and stand on the goal line.

'What's tha' up to?' the ref would say. 'I'm going to save this penalty,' said Muscle. 'How's tha' going to do that? Tha' can't use thi' hands tha' knows,' said the referee. 'I know that ref. I'm going to stop it wi' mi' 'ead,' said Muscle.

This would always prove too much for the penalty taker who, instead of keeping cool and placing the ball, would feel challenged to knock Muscle's head from his shoulders. Many tried but none succeeded. The inevitable result of aiming at a spot just between Muscle's eyes was that the ball ended up fifty yards behind the penalty taker.

Off the field he made a handsome living heading anything for money. For instance whenever the fair came to the village we'd all turn up at the coconut shy to win one for Muscle. Armed with our coconut he'd throw it high in the air and then head it. This act inevitably drew a large crowd and very soon we'd be going round the punters laying odds that Muscle could head the coconut three times running, and more than that, break it.

He never failed and was so good at it that the man who ran the coconut shy made a serious offer for Muscle to tour with him. All he had to do was stand in for the coconuts and let people throw things at his head, but he declined, saying he had better things to do. It was on the football field that he put his marvellous skull to the most effective use. He used his forehead not simply as a defensive weapon but often in an offensive role.

He was virtually unstoppable from dead-ball situations, launching himself at the ball like a guided missile, scattering opponents and heading goals from the most unlikely positions.

I'd not seen Muscle for ages, and then I went back home to visit an old friend. We'd had a night out supping a few and were walking back to our house when we saw a figure lying on the pavement. It was Muscle, drunk as a monkey. We picked him up and took him home. At least I took him to the house where he used to live when we were kids. The back door was open and we dumped him in the kitchen.

My friend who had led a life more sheltered than mine had not met Muscle before. 'Who is he?' he asked as we walked the damp streets home. 'He's an old mate. His name's Muscle Eadie,' I said. 'What's his claim to fame?' my friend asked. 'You're not going to believe this, but he heads coconuts,' I said.

'You've been away too long,' said my friend.

Skull Skill 2

George Best flew home one weekend for a change of underwear and I am one of the few people I know who does not find his behaviour baffling. This is because I have known for a long time that footballers are among the more eccentric members of our society. A lifetime observing Barnsley Football Club has satisfied me on that point.

I have written elsewhere of the centre-half who marked his debut by heading a spectacular hat trick of own goals and who, by the end of the season, was only a few goals behind the centre-forward as the club's top goal scorer. The crucial difference was that the centre-forward scored his goals against the opposition whereas the centre-half specialised in sticking them past his own goalkeeper.

However, thumbing back through the years, it is clear that the biggest eccentrics were to be found among the forwards, particularly those with a No. 9 on their backs. Barnsley had some splendid centre-forwards: Eddie McMorran, as brave as a bull, George Robledo, Tommy Taylor and the deadly Cec McCormack. It also had one or two whose extraordinary behaviour in every way compensated for their complete lack of ability.

Thinking about it nowadays, it is apparent that the reason why we had so many loony No. 9s as opposed to only the odd loony No. 7 or No. 5, was that unless you had exceptional ability, like Taylor or McCormack, you had to have a slate loose to earn a living spending Saturday afternoons in conflict with the likes of Sid Bycroft. Not blessed with the ability to beat Bycroft at playing football, the only answer was to try muscle and in those days centre-halves like Bycroft had muscles in their eyebrows. Ultimately, Barnsley's centre-forwards had to accept the role of kamikaze pilots – every Saturday they would take the field knowing that the best they could expect was a broken leg.

The most spectacular eccentric we ever had at Barnsley was a chunky, bald-headed fellow who was nicknamed 'Bullet' in honour of his exceptional ability at launching himself head first into a packed goal-mouth. Now in my day I have seen centre-forwards who have been both good in the air and on the floor, like Lawton, Chivers and Charles. I have seen centre-forwards who were good in the air only – Hateley, of the golden forehead, immediately springs to mind. Also I have seen centre-forwards who were useless in the air but magic on the carpet, like Cec McCormack and Charlie Wayman.

But never had I seen a centre-forward who was useless both in the air and on the ground until I saw the Bullet. Moreover, he was the only player I ever saw who was good with his head on the floor. Not even Muscle Eadie had this talent.

The Bullet was at his deadliest with his nose two inches from the deck, his body parallel to the turf and the sun glinting on his bald head. He lay there as if dead while the trainer ran on the field. My neighbour, who missed the incident, asked what had happened. 'Bullet got kicked,' said my old man. 'Where?' asked our neighbour. 'On his head,' said the old man. 'That's all right then,' said our neighbour and sure enough, the Bullet was soon revived. The man who kicked him on the head was taken from the field with a broken toe, but you can believe that if you want to.

What is true is that in the season he played for Barnsley, the Bullet scored about fifteen goals, and all of them went in off the top of his head in circumstances where normal players would have used the instep.

'at his deadliest with his nose two inches from the deck'

Equally curious was the way that Bullet arrived and departed the club. Legend had it that he was a local boy spotted while playing junior club soccer, but nobody I ever spoke to owned up to him. When he left after the season, he didn't go back to the local league, he wasn't sold, he wasn't given a free, he simply disappeared. I never saw him again – or did I? I'll tell you a funny story about that.

Some ten years after watching him from the terraces at Barnsley, I was travelling from London to Manchester by rail. As the train slowed on its approach to Manchester, we passed a football field where a game was taking place. As you do, I immediately looked for a bit of action, and as our train passed slowly behind the goals the winger crossed low into the goalmouth, there was a flash of shiny skull and the ball was in the net. Only one man could score goals like that. Was it, could it be? Tantalisingly, the train passed the ground. I pressed against the window to see the better, but the scorer was lying on the floor slightly concussed and surrounded by admiring team mates. Just like the Bullet used to be.

I considered pulling the communication cord, but decided against it. I could imagine the conversation I'd have with the conductor. 'You see, I thought I saw an old friend. He was lying stunned on the floor after having headed a goal that a normal person would have kicked into goal. His name is Bullet and he used to play for Barnsley.' 'Certainly, sir, just sit still and the green van will be here in a minute.'

Given I have witnessed all that I have just written about, you can see why I curl my lip sardonically whenever anyone comments on George Best's 'extraordinary' behaviour. Having seen a man earn a living by putting his head where other men would not dare put a steel-shod boot, why should I be amazed at someone who flies 2000 miles merely to change his underpants.

Necessary Screwballs

Goalkeepers, like things that go bump in the night, defy analysis. They are as much a mystery in the general order of things as the function of the human appendix. It is, of course, relatively easy to explain what they have to do: their purpose is to prevent the ball entering the net by any means at their disposal, namely by catching it, punching it, kicking it, heading it or, if they so desire, throwing their caps at it. The mystery lies in the fact that this seemingly simple, straightforward task produces people of incredibly complex and often eccentric personality. Even today, when the game appears to be played by robots, when individuality is ruthlessly stifled at birth, the goalkeeper has survived with all his personal idiosyncracies intact. No one knows better than goalkeepers themselves that the price they pay for their freedom is to be talked about behind their backs. In the totalitarian regime of modern-day soccer they are treated as necessary screwballs. Because of this it is a commonly held belief that all goalkeepers have a slate loose, that the nature of the job being what it is a man must be barmy to do it. The other theory is that the goalkeeper, because he is custodian of the most important part of a football field, slowly develops into a paranoiac.

I suspect that Clakker May would be regarded as a classic example by those people who reckon all goalkeepers are born crazy. You'd never suspect there was anything wrong by looking at him. He was a tall, stringy, quiet youth who lived with his parents and ten brothers and sisters in a council house near the pit gates. He became our goalkeeper quite by chance. One day we were a man short, and Len, our trainer, asked Clakker to play in goal. The result was a revelation. It wasn't so much when he donned the jersey he changed in his attitude towards his team-mates, it was simply that he believed that the rules of the game related to everyone except himself.

We became aware of his quirk the first time he touched the ball. He left his goal line to meet a hard, high cross, caught the ball cleanly, shaped to clear downfield, and then, for no apparent reason, spun round and fled to the back of the net. This move dumbfounded players, officials and spectators alike. As we stood gaping, Clakker ran from the back of the net and booted the ball over the halfway line. Nobody moved as it bounced aimlessly towards the opposite goal and then the referee broke the silence by blowing on his whistle and pointing to the centre spot. This appeared to upset Clakker.

'What's tha' playin' at?' he asked the referee.

'I was just about to ask thee same question,' said the referee. By this time Len had run on to the field.

'What the bloody hell . . .' he began.

'Nay, Len. Tha' sees I caught this ball and then I looks up and I saw this big centre forrard coming at me and I thought, "Bugger this lot", so I got out of his way,' Clakker explained.

'Tha' ran into t'bloody net wi' t'ball and tha' scored,' Len shouted.

'Scored,' said Clakker, incredulously.

'Scored,' said Len emphatically.

Clakker shook his head. Len tried to keep calm. 'Look, lad,' he said putting his arm round Clakker's shoulders, 'I know it's thi' first game and all that, but tha' must get one thing straight. When tha' catches t'ball gi' it some clog downfield. Whatever tha' does don't run into t'net.'

Clakker nodded.

But it made little difference. In the next twenty minutes Clakker ran into the net thirteen times and we were losing 14–2. At this point the referee intervened. He called us all together and said: 'Na' look, lads, this is making mock of a great game. If it goes on like this t'scoor will be in t'hundreds and I'll have to mek a report to t'League Management Committee and there'll be hell to play.' We all nodded in agreement. The referee thought a bit and then said: 'What we'll do is amend t'rules. If Clakker runs into t'back of t'net in future it won't count as a goal, allus providin' he caught t'ball on t'right side of t'line in t'first place.'

Everyone agreed and play continued with this extraordinary amendment to the rules. At the final whistle we had lost fifteen five and Clakker had shown that apart from his eccentric interpretation of the rules he was a remarkably good goalkeeper. Nobody said much after the game. It seemed useless to ask Clakker what went wrong because all of us agreed that like all goalkeepers he was a bit screwy. Our theory was confirmed by Clakker's old man, who when told of his son's extraordinary behaviour simply shook his head and said, 'He allus was a bit potty'.

But that was not the end of Clakker's career, not quite. He was picked for the next game because we didn't want to hurt him too much. Len, the trainer, called us together on the night before the game and explained how we might curb Clakker's madness. His plan was that the defenders should close in behind Clakker whenever he went out for a ball and bar his way into the net. Any resistance from Clakker should be firmly dealt with and if possible the ball taken from him and cleared upfield. In case Clakker should break through his own rearguard Len had taken the precaution of hiding the nets. His theory was that provided Clakker ran into goal, but straight out again, the referee would be unable to decide what had happened.

The reports of our last game had attracted a large crowd to the ground for Clakker's second appearance. All his family were present to see if it was true what people were saying about Clakker's extraordinary behaviour.

Things worked quite well for a time. Every time Clakker caught the ball we fell in around him and urged him away from his goal. Once he escaped us and nipped into goal, but he had the sense to escape immediately around the goalpost and clear downfield. The referee looked puzzled for a minute and gave Clakker a peculiar look, but did not give a goal because he could not believe what he thought he saw. We were leading two goals to nil with five minutes of the first half left when Clakker gave the game away. Over-confident at having duped the referee once before, he ran over his own goal line with the ball. His plan came to grief when he collided with the iron stanchion at the back of the goal. As he staggered drunkenly against the support the referee blew for a goal and gave Clakker the sort of look that meant all was now revealed.

When half time came none of us could look forward to the next forty-five minutes with any optimism. Len came on the field and beckoned myself and the centre half to one side. 'Na' look, lads, we've got to do something about yon Clakker,' he said. 'I've thought about playing him out of goal, but that's too dangerous. I can't just take him off because yon referee wouldn't allow it. So there's only one thing we can do.' He paused and looked at both of us.

'What's that?' I asked.

'Fix him?' said Len.

'Fix him?' I said.

Len nodded. 'When you get a chance, and as soon as you can, clobber him. I don't want him to get up, either.'

The centre half was smiling.

'Look,' I said to him, 'we can't clobber our own team-mate. It's not done.'

He looked at me pityingly. 'Leave it to me,' he said. 'I've fixed nicer people than Clakker.'

It took two minutes of the second half for Clakker to get fixed. There was a scrimmage in our goalmouth and when the dust had cleared Clakker lay prostrate on his goal line. Len came running on to the field, trying to look concerned. The centre half was trying hard to look innocent. Clakker's father had drifted over to the scene and was looking down at his son's body. 'He's better like that,' he said.

Len said to him, 'Tek your Clakker home and don't let him out till t'game's finished.'

Clakker's old man nodded and signalled to some of his sons to pick Clakker up. The last we saw of them they were carrying Clakker out of the field and home. We did quite well without him and managed to win. Afterwards in the dressing room some of the lads were wondering how Clakker became injured. Len said: 'Tha' nivver can tell wi' goalkeepers. It's quite likely he laid himself out.'

Clakker had a profound effect on me. Since that day many years ago when he was persuaded out of the game I have never been able to watch a football match without spending a great deal of the time wondering what was going on underneath the goalkeeper's cap. None of the goalkeepers I have ever seen in first-class football could hold a candle to Clakker, but most of them from time to time have revealed flashes of rare individuality. Bradford Park Avenue once had a goalkeeper called Chick Farr who thought nothing of racing far out of his goal area, tackling an opposing forward and racing off downfield like a demented Stanley Matthews. Whenever his little fantasy was interrupted by a successful tackle Farr would gallop back to his goal line, from time to time casting fearful glances over his shoulder like a man being pursued by a ghost. Farr's other party piece was strictly illegal. When he could not be bothered to save a high shot he would reach nonchalantly above his head and pull the cross-bar down. Faced with the inevitable telling off from a referee, Farr would pull his cap down over his eyes and try his best to look gormless. His act was a convincing one, not because he was born that way, but because like every goalkeeper he had become expert in hiding his folly. Occasionally, however, the stresses of the occupation become too much for some goalkeepers and they crack up. Sometimes it happens in public, as with the recent case of a First Division goalkeeper who showed his displeasure of the way the crowd was criticising his goalkeeping by taking his shorts down and showing a large part of his backside to the terraces. At least this particular goalkeeper relieved himself in one great, spectacular gesture. The majority of his kind spend years suffering between the posts, whipping boys for the mob at the back of the goal, sacrifices to the inefficiency of their team-mates. I watched one goalkeeper at Barnsley suffer this way through many seasons. He came to the club fit and virile and stuffed with confidence. When he left on a free transfer he had shrunk inside his green jersey, his nerves were destroyed, they even rumoured that his wife had left him. I often wondered what became of him and discovered the truth some time later when I was doing a story about a building site. I was talking football with the foreman when he asked me if I remembered the goalkeeper. I said I did and the foreman said he was working on the site.

'Where is he?' I asked.

'Up theer,' said the foreman, pointing towards heaven.

'Where exactly,' I enquired, hoping he wasn't trying to be funny.

'On top of yon chimney,' said the foreman.

I peered up, and there, high in the sky, sitting on top of the chimney was the goalkeeper.

'He seems to like it up theer. Can't get him down until it's knockin'-off time,' said the foreman.

I thought there might be a story in it, so I asked the foreman if I might interview the goalkeeper.

He shrugged. 'He's a funny bugger, but I'll try.'

He cupped his hands to his mouth and bellowed at the top of the chimney, 'Alf, theers a reporter down 'ere what wants to interview thi abart goalkeepin'.'

There was a long silence. Nothing stirred on the top of the chimney for a while and then the figure turned and looked down. And down the miles of silence separating us floated the reply:

'Tell him to get stuffed.'

The foreman shrugged and said, 'I told you. He's a rum feller. Still, I always think tha's got to be a bit strange to be a goalkeeper.'

I've often wondered since what kind of peace the goalkeeper discovered on top of that chimney, and wondered also what kind of revenge he was planning on the people below who had driven him there. I don't think he was potty or excessively anti-social. It was simply that he, like every goalkeeper, knew what it was like to be one of the world's most abused minority group.

Closet Wingers

It is an axiom of the modern game of football that wingmen, like people who thatch roofs and make clogs, are a dying breed. It is remarkable that a country whose one certain contribution to the international history of football is Stanley Matthews should now seem intent on pretending that he never existed.

Once upon a time in the days when footballers wore shorts to their knees and were shod in boots with bulging toe-caps the sight of the wingman improvising his talents down the touchline, delighting and disappointing in turn, was a commonplace on the football fields of Britain. Wingmen were the temperamental artists whose performance was controlled by the state of the moon, or the horoscope in that morning's *Daily Mirror* or more simply by the fact of whether or not they felt like playing well. They were the only members of a side who were allowed the luxury of personal eccentricity by the fans. I once played with a winger who wore a flat cap and woollen mittens on days when the weather was bad. Neither his teammates, opponents nor spectators ever remarked on his curious attire because he was a wingman. Had he been a centre half or a full back he would immediately have been marked down as a weirdo of some sort and asked to mend his ways or retire from the game.

In those dear departed days the best wingmen were always referred to as closet wingers. It grew out of the days when we had the best team in the Barnsley and District Backyard League. Our success depended mainly on an unbeaten home record which was achieved by the efforts of our right winger, Albert, and a long row of outside toilets or closets as they were more commonly known.

Albert was an absolute master at charging down the wing and, when challenged by the opposing defenders, flicking the ball against the toilet door and collecting the rebound. The only time he was shown to fail was on the occasion when the occupant of the toilet opened the door in time to take one of Albert's passes in the midriff.

Albert became well known locally as Geronimo, the closet winger. The Geronimo tag had nothing to do with his footballing ability but derived from his hatred of water and hair-cuts which created an appearance to remind us all of the Indians we saw on the screen at the local flea-pit. In those days our tactics were simple and effective. At every conceivable opportunity we would feed the ball to Geronimo, who was invariably lurking by his beloved closets, and away he would go, flicking the ball against the toilet doors, racing on to the rebound and repeating the act until he had cleared the whole defence.

For a couple of seasons we were unbeatable and Albert the closet winger became a local personality. Inevitably it couldn't last for ever and the slide downhill for both Albert and the

'opened the door in time to take one of Albert's passes in the midriff'

team came on the day we met the Klondyke. The team was so named because the part of the village it represented put one in mind of a frontier town during the gold-rush. To describe them as hard opponents would be doing them an injustice. Ferocious is a more accurate description.

It must also be remembered that in the Backyard League there was no referee to penalise dirty play. The simple ethic therefore was: 'If kicked say nothing, but wait and kick back.' Also in these games we did without the normal post-match formalities like shaking hands and congratulating the other chap. Any team which beat the fearsome Klondyke realised that when the game ended the sensible tactic was to race home immediately because any attempt at the normal courtesies would undoubtedly mean a free ride to the local out-patients department.

It was in this frame of mind we began our epic encounter. All went reasonably well until Albert began his first run down the wing. In and out of the defence he went, flicking the ball on to the toilet doors, the rebound magically dropping at his twinkling feet. With the Klondyke defence nonplussed he shot home the first goal.

The Klondyke team, for all the fact that it included many players with surprisingly narrow foreheads and close-set eyes, were not short on swift answers when faced with a problem like this. The next time that Albert set off on one of his runs we were made aware of the Klondyke genius for tactical improvisation. As Albert twinkle-toed along the toilets, the Klondyke full back, built like a brick brewery, began a diagonal run towards him. As he reached Albert he didn't stop to challenge, he didn't hesitate to decide which way the winger was going, he just kept running as if his target was somewhere on the horizon beyond Albert's right shoulder. The noise of impact, of bone on bone, was terrible, and followed immediately by the sound of splintering wood as Albert, the full back and the ball smashed through one of the green toilet doors. We peered inside and the wreckage was awful.

Albert and the full back lay at peace on the floor, surrounded by fragments of wood and jagged pieces of what is politely termed sanitary ware. We picked them up and revived them and then had to abandon the match because the owner of the toilet turned up on his daily visit and when he saw the damage went to fetch the police. We never played there again because the law warned us off and some time later the council pulled the toilets down along with the houses they belonged to. The inhabitants were shipped out to a new estate with inside toilets and a better view of the pit. Albert went with his parents to the new estate, but he was never the same winger without a row of closets. After a couple of months in his new environment Albert went into premature retirement in a remand home for stealing lead. But he had made his mark. Whenever we saw a good winger he was always a 'closet winger'.

It is easy to scoff at closet wingers, but in fact they have made a colourful contribution to our game. What is more significant, it was a closet winger who unwittingly decided the future of English football. As is generally known, it was Sir Alf Ramsey who killed off the old romantic notion of wingmen. In Ramsey's team of workers there was no place for the eccentric or the whimsical. It was a beautiful machine and it didn't need adorning with frills. Now contrary to general opinion Sir Alf's plan for wingmen did not occur because he simply happened to think about it one day while taking a bath. It is my theory that his scheme for the liquidation of wingmen had lurked in his mind for some considerable time and had its roots in some kind of deep emotional upset. Which is where a closet winger called Johnny Kelly comes in.

He was a left-winger of genius who played for Barnsley in the early fifties. A shy, square sturdy man with the slightly bandy legs that are the hallmark of all great wingers.

I don't know if you've ever considered the remarkable fact that bandy legs are an asset to most sportsmen. That they help people who ride horses is a thought too obvious to need explanation. But it is not generally known that they greatly assist cricketers also. I once played in a cricket team with a man who possessed the most splendid pair of hooped legs I have yet seen.

As a batsman he was particularly skilled in the art of back play. Now this technique was generally suicidal in the league in which we played where the umpires worked strictly to licensing hours and granted leg-before-wicket appeals with increasing regularity as opening time approached. In this situation my bandy-legged friend was the only batsman in the league to play back and prosper. Whenever struck on his superbly bowed legs and appealed against he would simply point to the gap between his limbs, through which all three stumps were clearly visible, and say to the umpire in his most pained voice: 'Leg before wicket with a pair of bloody legs like mine?' No umpire, no matter how thirsty, dare give him out!

I digress only in the interests of science and humanity. It is time someone pointed out the virtues of playing sport on a pair of bandy legs. No one who has them should feel unhappy so long as they always remember to play back.

Which returns us to Alf Ramsey, because those of you with long memories will doubtless recall that he also used to play back – full back, that is – and very good he was too. But he was no good against bandy-legged wingers, as Johnny Kelly proved. Kelly was the kind of winger you don't see around nowadays. A player of skill and original wit. The sort of wing-man who exploded theories, not expounded them. He played only once for Scotland, which was an act of criminal neglect on a player who must have been the best Scottish winger of his day. That he was ignored has obviously to do with the fact that he played for Barnsley. The selectors in Glasgow obviously thought they played in the Isthmian League. A great pity, because he had the kind of unique skill that should have been spread before multitudes and not just the faithful 15,000 who used to watch Barnsley in his day.

Still, it does mean that there were 14,999 other people who will swear to what I am going to tell you now. They and I were present that important day, many years ago, when Alf Ramsey suffered the trauma that changed his life and put the skids under wingers. He was playing right back for Southampton at the time, an urbane, immaculate footballer who seemed as out of place at Barnsley as a bowler hat in a pawnshop.

In this particular game Johnny Kelly had one of those days when all his genius flowed into his feet. If you have ever seen Matthews or Finney or Georgie Best at their finest then you'll know what I mean. He flicked his hips and Ramsey sat down in wonderment. He waved his foot over the ball like a wand, daring Ramsey to guess what might happen next, and as the full back anticipated a move outside, Kelly came inside and left him for dead. At one stage he demonstrated his complete mastery by beating Ramsey, waiting for him to recover and then beating him again. Had Kelly been on the Southampton side and doing this to certain of the Barnsley defenders he would have had his impudence rewarded with a bed in the nearest emergency ward. But Ramsey played it clean and endeavoured to look as dignified as any man can when he is having his nose rubbed in the dirt.

The crowd didn't help. They relished the sight of Kelly shredding Ramsey's reputation. This, remember, was in the days when footballers were the victims of individual abuse and not the collective sort they get from today's rehearsed choirs. Thus the comments, though not so loud, were more personal and biting.

My theory is that as Alf Ramsey sat in that dressing room in Barnsley, scraping the mud from his boots and his reputation, he first thought of his revenge on wingers. He didn't want just Kelly's scalp, but the destruction of the whole tricky race.

It's not a bad theory, particularly when you consider what happened to Alf Ramsey and that Johnny Kelly was last heard of manufacturing a liquid bleach. It's an even stronger theory when you realise that wingers like Kelly are now more rare than five-legged giraffes.

But I have cornered whatever consolation there is left to people who loved the game in the dear, daft days before Mr Ramsey got his paws on it. When I read of the experts trying to explain to themselves just what he was up to, and why, I sat there giggling gently to myself, nursing my memories, thinking fondly of a grey afternoon many seasons ago when a closet winger with bandy legs and baggy shorts made a monkey of a master mind.

Memories are made of . . .

Great inside forwards, like blissful marriages, are made in heaven. They are fashioned out of gold and sent on earth to win football matches and weave the stuff that memories are made of. Their deeds are branded on the mind. They are the architects who design a game, the artists who adorn it. Wingmen are more spectacular, centre halves more pugnacious, goalkeepers more idiosyncratic, but inside forwards, like leg-spin bowlers, are the connoisseur's delight.

My first clear memory of football is of a great inside forward at work. His name was Horatio Carter and I don't know how old I was when I first laid eyes on him, but I do remember that it was in the days when he played with Sunderland and he came to Barnsley and I stood on a tin can to see over the heads of the spectators in front of me. He strode alone on to the field some time after the other players, as if disdaining their company, as if to underline that his special qualities were worthy of a separate entrance. The Barnsley fans gave him the sort of reception they reserved for visiting dignitaries. You know the sort of thing: 'Big 'ed' and 'Get your bleedin' hair cut, Sybil'.

He treated the crowd and the game with a massive disdain, as if the whole affair was far beneath his dignity. He showed only one speck of interest in the proceedings, but it was decisive. The scores were level with only a few minutes to go when Carter, about thirty yards from the Barnsley goal and with his back to it, received a fast, wild cross. He killed it in mid-air with his right foot and as it dropped spun round and hit an alarming left-foot volley into the roof of the Barnsley goal. At least after he was seen to kick the ball it was seen to appear in the net, but no one on the ground, least of all the Barnsley goalkeeper, could say just how it arrived there. Carter didn't wait to see where the ball went. He knew. He continued his spin through 180 degrees and strolled back to the halfway line as if nothing had happened. Normally the Barnsley crowd greeted any goal by the opposition with a loud silence, but as Carter reached the halfway line a rare thing happened. Someone shouted: 'I wish we'd got eleven like thee, Carter lad.' The great player allowed himself a thin smile, as well he might, for he never received a greater accolade than that. In the following years I saw him whenever I could, first with Derby County, where with Peter Doherty he made up the most attractive and deadly pair of inside forwards possessed by any club side in post-war England. Then in his later years I watched him give his spectacular one-man show with Hull City. The sight of one man conducting the fortunes of his team is the most warming spectacle in football. It's an heroic situation in which the individual takes on the awesome qualities of the silent stranger in the cowboy film, the man who rides slowly into town and plugs all the baddies. Carter's performance at Hull contained all the heroic qualities, but they were embellished by the man's sense of showmanship. During the course of his weekly demonstrations of the art of football to the citizens of Hull, Carter took all the corners, all the free kicks, all the throw-ins, and, of course, all the penalties. Such was his domination that when one arrived at the ground one half expected to see Carter at the turnstile taking the gate money.

From the moment I first saw him at Barnsley, Carter became the first player in my World XI to meet the Outer Galaxies. The curious thing about the team, which proves what I say about inside forwards, is that eventually the forward line consisted of three inside rights and two inside lefts: Horatio Carter, Len Shackleton, Ernie Taylor, Bobby Charlton and Steve Griffiths.

Of that bunch only Griffiths is unknown, but he was a marvellous footballer. I suppose in the few years he played with Barnsley he gave me more delight and taught me more about the inside forward's art than any other player. He learnt his skills in the South Yorkshire coalfield in the days when, if Barnsley were short of a player, they simply whistled down the pit shaft and took the first man up. Today if they whistled at the pit top the chances are they'd get a bass guitarist for a pop group.

Griffiths played for a while with Portsmouth, and then, after the war, returned to Barnsley for the epilogue of his career. In those last few seasons he showed us all his repertoire. He was a slight man, with a thin, sad face and slender, slightly bowed legs. Dressed in an ankle-length overcoat, muffler and cap, he became the sort of figure you see standing outside betting shops in Yorkshire pit villages. No one looked less like an athlete, but this was part of his deception. He would shamble round the field looking preoccupied and lost, like a man who suddenly remembers he has left the tap running at home.

But the moment he received the ball you detected his skill. Like all great footballers he could take a ball from any angle and lay it quietly dead at his feet. I can see him now, quite clearly, shoulders hunched, the ball at his feet, standing in mid-field, moving this way and that, tormenting the defenders, challenging them to anticipate his ideas, torturing the crowd into screaming 'Get rid, get rid'. And always at the point where even I, his dearest fan, was damning him for a fool, when the defence seemed to have been allowed time to build an impregnable wall, he would move. A quick body swerve past the man marking him, a shuffle, a change of feet and a thirty-yard ball trimming the turf to drop like a dead bird into the full stride of the wingman.

Griffiths was generous with his colleagues. When Tommy Taylor, that fine centre forward so tragically killed in the Munich air disaster, first came into the Barnsley team it was Griffiths who nursed him through his growing pains. In one game he gave Taylor a goal with a stunning gesture. He set off dribbling through the defence and by the time he reached the goalkeeper the field behind was littered with bodies. Griffiths taunted the goalkeeper into a fruitless dive, walked the ball round him, trapped it on the line and beckoned Taylor to come and push the ball into the net. He retired soon after and I missed him sorely.

The Voice in the Crowd

Every Saturday, when Barnsley were at home we'd pick up Arthur by the bottom boozer and take him to the match – a little furry man who sat in the back of the car in a quivering silence like a bespectacled mouse while the old man continued his monologue about how Barnsley would pulverise Rotherham.

The old man reckoned he was henpecked and had a helluva life with his missus. You could imagine it to look at him. He was put on earth to be everybody's rubbing rag. But he changed dramatically once he got to the ground.

Having paid his half-crown and settled on his favourite concrete step behind the goals, he became a fearsome mixture of R.S.M. Brittain and King Kong. He undoubtedly possessed the loudest voice ever owned by a human being, and this, coupled with an actor's sense of timing, made him a star attraction at Barnsley's home games.

He wasn't a witty phrase-maker, he didn't believe in the devastating aside, but his bellowed advice of 'Get stuck in' or 'Get rid' or 'Let him bloody rot' had the simple effectiveness of a battering ram. He wasn't unique. In those days every team had its Arthur, the belligerent customer who demanded value for his money and roared like a wounded animal when he thought he was being sold short. Today things are different. The art of barracking has lost its individual voice and has been replaced with massed choirs singing silly songs. Today angry dissatisfaction is expressed not with a bellow of pain but by a toilet roll curling upwards from the Spion Kop, thrown by a yobbo who can't think of anything to say.

The reasons for this change in social behaviour are for someone else to explore, but the effect of the change saddens me. The lack of individual voice means a loss of personal identity. Crowds today speak with the same tongue no matter who they are supporting.

Football choirs throughout Britain all sing the same pop song, whether it be in praise of Millwall or Southport, and even when a resourceful group breaks through with something unique and personal, such as Liverpool's 'Ee-aye-addio', it soon becomes adopted nationally.

Where today are those strong, loud voices of individual protest, the Arthurs who every Saturday found that the Kop was their stage, where they broke free from nagging wives and bum bailiffs and for ninety minutes told the world and their fellow men exactly what they thought about them?

Barracking today has become the opposite of what it was intended to be. It is now a form of sing-song employed by spectators to entertain themselves when they are bored, instead of being the barb to goad the players and the spectators into new life.

That marvellous writer H. D. Davies would be horrified by today's crowds. He was the first football writer to spot the value of the lone persistent voice from the Kop. A few weeks before his tragic death Don Davies recorded the judgement of one critic at Maine Road on a winger who fancied himself as another Matthews.

After a thwarted attempt to weave his way through the opposing defence the winger was assessed by one spectator thus: 'Look at 'im trying to dribble. Why doesn't he learn? He's got nothin' else to do.'

Cricket, too, is suffering from much the same malaise as soccer. What it lacks today is the individual flash of perceptive barracking that means so much to the game. In Yorkshire and Lancashire, where this tradition was born, each team, whether it be the county side or the local XI, would have at least one outspoken critic whose self-appointed job was to scourge both locals and visitors alike.

Barnsley Cricket Club had such a spectator who every home game, no matter what the conditions, would sit, wrapped in a large brown raincoat, by one side of the sight-screen bellowing advice. No one escaped him. He was particularly fond of baiting our captain, a spiky old professional with a brittle temper.

On one occasion we were being trounced by the visiting team, and every time the ball flashed through our captain's defensive field placings for yet another boundary the man by the sight-screen would bellow, 'Put a bloody man theer.'

This went on for some time, until finally the skipper could

bear it no longer. As the ball raced yet again to the boundary he stood with hands on hips facing his accuser and awaiting the inevitable. It came: 'Put a bloody man theer.' Our captain went purple and bawled across the field, 'How many men does tha' think I've got, sithee?' A pause, then back came the hoarse reply, 'Not bloody sufficient.'

Their feud was a constant feature of our games, and I believe in the end they became quite fond of one another. Their most memorable repartee occurred one day when we were faced with a large score on a very wet wicket and had decided to play for a draw. The captain tried to assure the result by wasting as much time as possible.

After every ball he would go down the wicket and indulge in extensive gardening. Being a fairly violent man by nature, he did not tap the divots back but thumped them into position with a resounding noise. He had just completed one of his sessions and was strolling back to his crease when the critic spoke.

'Ayup,' he bellowed. The captain turned to face him and shouted back, 'And what's tha' want?' The critic rose from his seat and replied, 'Tha' wants to be careful wi' all that thumpin', there's men workin' under theer.'

The captain and his critic have long since departed and there is nothing in their place except silence. I'll bet Don Davies's man at Maine Road now spends his Saturday afternoons in the betting shop. The sadness of it all, the quantity of loss, was made apparent to me the other day when talking to a friend of mine who in his youth supported Chesterfield. He recalled the great days, but the interesting point was that he remembered the vitality and agitation of the crowd as much as the deeds of his heroes.

One of his recollections will serve as an epitaph to the disappearing barracker. Chesterfield at the time had a fine inside forward called Tommy Capel, whose brother also played at full back. It was generally supposed by the Spion Kop fraternity that the full back made the side because of his brother's skill.

This feeling was given expression after one game, a cup-tie at Chesterfield, which the home team desperately needed to win. With the scores level and one minute to go Chesterfield were awarded a penalty. The kick was entrusted to the full back, the mistrusted brother. This unfortunate fellow took the penalty and not only missed by a mile but suffered the indignity of seeing his shot hit the scoreboard.

There was a stunned silence from the home fans, broken eventually by a lone voice from the Kop which, with immense dignity and suffering, declared, 'It's bloody nepotism, that's what it is, bloody nepotism.'

'"Tha' wants to be careful wi' all that thumpin', there's men workin' under theer."'

The Week Charlie Won the Pools

The minute Charlie Blake knew he had 24 points on the pools he nipped straight out to the Club where he borrowed fifty pounds from Len the steward until the next week when he would receive that nice fat cheque from some smooth, young pools official at a posh hotel.

After he'd got his fifty he came straight to the spitting ring at the Top Boozer to find a few of his mates. There were about six of us there and we calculated that the 24 points ought to be worth about £50,000. So we started celebrating where we were, continued in the Bottom Boozer and ended up in the concert room at the New Boozer.

There was a stripper on that night, a big, overblown girl from Sheffield. And when she heard the news she came and sat at our table and started downing gallons of cherry brandy. Every time Charlie asked her if she wanted another drink she gave him a long smoochy look and said, 'Well, I won't say no'.

Charlie was soon well away. He was throwing his money round like it was Barnsley Feast Week or something. He was taken home by a stranger in a car who carefully lifted what was left of the fifty quid, plonked Charlie on his doorstep and had enough decency to knock up Charlie's old woman before he drove off.

She hauled Charlie to bed and then went through his pockets. She found about ten bob in loose change. Next morning Charlie swore that his old woman had pinched his money. Normally it would have been an accurate guess. But this time someone had beaten the old woman to it. Anyway there was a row and Charlie's old woman told him that when he got the money he had better put it all in the bank and keep it there because if she ever got her hands on it she would pack her bags and be away to their Elsie's in Sheffield.

Charlie nipped out earlier than usual for his drink that night. He went straight to the New Boozer and asked Bill the manager if he could borrow fifty. He got the money without any trouble, which was remarkable because normally when it came to helping out with a few quid Bill was about as much use as a chocolate bobby. But I suppose he reckoned that he would get it back, and with plenty of interest too, because it was odds on that the brewery would have to go on overtime when Charlie got that cheque of his.

This night wasn't much different from the night before except there were possibly more people drinking Charlie's money away. A busload from Bradford even got tight at Charlie's expense and when the bloke who sells bags of shrimps and cockles came into the concert room Charlie bought the lot including the basket.

Miss Cherry Brandy came and drank with us again and later Charlie got a bit amorous and started dancing with her. She was two feet taller than Charlie and twice as ugly but he held her tight like she was Betty Grable. He clung to her so ardently that she must have been relieved when the drink reached his legs and he went to sleep on the floor.

His mates took him home this time and delivered Charlie and what was left of his fifty quid to his old woman. If she went through his pockets she was unlucky again because he must have spent the best part of what he had borrowed that night.

When we got to the pit next morning the gaffer man told us Charlie Blake had retired. He had sent a note to the pit saying that because he had won the pools he had decided to give up pit work and buy a business instead. 'Lucky him,' the gaffer said. It just about summed up the feelings of us all. Somebody brought a morning paper down the pit and the dividends said that 24 points paid £55,000. No wonder Charlie retired.

But knowing Charlie, a lot of thought went into his decision to give up work altogether. He had been a miner for nearly forty years and was a good pitman. He knew more about every aspect of coal production than any of these fancy young fellows from college who come down nowadays with their little white certificates which say they are the gaffer.

He had worked hard in the grim days to bring his kids up, and even if he and the old woman acted a bit like Mr and Mrs Andy Capp they seemed to enjoy that kind of love-hate relationship. Again, if he did go to the club most nights and have a pint of two, gossip, play crib, dommies or snooker at least he wasn't screwed into the television set watching *Coronation Street*.

Charlie didn't turn up at the boozer that night but the regulars were full of his good fortune. We all agreed the only thing wrong was that he ought to have won it when he was a bit younger, before he got his lungs full of coaldust and his back covered in blue scars. But still it must be nice to retire before you are sixty-five, and, better still, to be in a position to tell the Coal Board where to put that framed certificate it issues to every miner with more than twenty years' 'meritorious service'.

Next morning when we came up from the day shift there was a notice pinned on the wall of the baths. It said, simply, 'Charlie Blake will be starting work on Monday'. Well, we all thought the money had turned him soft or something. But then the gaffer man told us what had happened. It appears Charlie had made a mistake checking his coupon. Instead of 24 points he only had 23 and the dividend was thirty-five bob.

That night in the New Boozer, Bill the manager looked about as cheerful as a pit pony. He would have to wait a long time for his money. But he got little sympathy from us. He could afford to lose the odd few quid, but Charlie couldn't.

So we decided to have a whip round the concert room for Charlie Blake. Most people who knew him put something in the hat – even the stripper – and we collected about £10, which was something. No one would volunteer to take the money round to Charlie's place because we were all too embarrassed for him. We couldn't leave it behind the bar for Charlie to collect because our William would get his great maulers on it, so we decided to give it to him the following Monday when he started work.

It was only ten quid and he would still owe another ninety. It might just as well have been £90,000 for all the chance Charlie would have of paying it back. But after a few more drinks we all decided we had done the proper thing by Charlie Blake. After all it was his mistake and there was nothing we could do about it . . . was there?

Skinner

Cup-ties were different from other games. If Barnsley won we went to the pictures in the best seats, but if they lost there was sometimes a punch-up and the old man would come home from the boozer with a skinful saying the beer was off.

Barnsley, of course, used to be a good cup-fighting side. They only won the Cup once and that was in 1912, but they've never forgotten it and many a team from a higher division has been slain by them on that ground with the muck stacks peeping over the paddock. The reason for Barnsley's success in the Cup was, more often than not, that their game remained unchanged throughout years of tactical innovation. The team was both blind and deaf to subtleties like the bolt defence, the wall pass, 4–2–4 and deep-lying centre forwards. Their game was founded rock solid on two basic principles best summed up by the exhortations of their supporters to 'Get stuck in' or, alternatively, 'Get rid'.

During one spectacular cup run after the war, when Barnsley had beaten a First Division side, the old man held forth on the team's virtues on the bus going home. What he said was: 'They'll take some stopping, yon team. They'll kick 'owt that moves.' The bus agreed.

This love of hard combative graft above all else was not in any way unique among the supporters who Saturday after Saturday had their week-end mood dictated by how their team fared. Their unanimous favourites were the hard men who got stuck in and got rid without thought for the game's niceties. The odd sophisticates who crept into the team were tolerated but never loved. Thus they will tell you even now that Danny Blanchflower once played for Barnsley, but that he wasn't a patch on Skinner Normanton.

Normanton, I suppose, personified Barnsley's cup-fighting qualities. He was tough, tireless, aggressive, with a tackle as swift and spectacular as summer lightning. In the family tree of football his grandfather was Wilf Copping, his godson is Nobby Stiles. And just in case anyone is still uncertain about what kind of player he was, he could claim a distant link with Rocky Marciano. He was a miner and built like one. Billiard-table legs and a chest like the front of a coal barge. He was so fearsome that there are those who will tell you that naughty children in and around Barnsley were warned by their parents, 'If you don't be good we'll send for Skinner.'

The other legend about him, probably equally true, was that certain inside forwards of delicate constitution were known to develop nervous rashes and mysterious stomach disorders when faced with the prospect of a Saturday afternoon's sport with Skinner in opposition.

Cup-ties were his speciality, inside forwards with international reputations were his meat. He clinched one game for Barnsley in a manner all his very own. There was about ten minutes to go, the scores level, and Barnsley were awarded a penalty. The inside forward placed the ball on the spot and as he turned to walk back Skinner, from the halfway line, set off running. The inside forward, ready to turn to take the kick, saw Skinner approaching like an odds-on favourite and wisely stepped aside. From that moment the grey, dour ground was lit with the purple and gold of pure fantasy. Without slackening speed Skinner kicked the ball with his toe-end. And, as he did, many things happened: the bar started shaking and humming, the goalkeeper fell to his face stunned and the ball appeared magically in the back of the net. What in fact had happened was that Skinner's shot had struck the underside of the crossbar, rebounded on to the back of the goalkeeper's neck, flattened him and ricocheted into the goal.

Barnsley, by virtue of Skinner's genius in scoring with the penalty and at the same time reducing the opponents to ten men, won the game.

It was soon after, though, that Skinner for the first and last time met his match. Again it was a cup-tie and this time Barnsley were playing Arsenal at Highbury. Going down on the train with the crates of light ale under the seat, we agreed that if Skinner could frighten them Barnsley had a chance. But we didn't know that Arsenal had someone just as hard as Skinner and twice as clever. His name was Alec Forbes and Barnsley lost. Going sadly home, we agreed with the thought that if Barnsley had Forbes they'd soon get into the First Division. What we left unsaid was that they'd probably make it by default because other teams faced with the prospect of playing against a side containing both Skinner and Forbes would probably give Barnsley two points to stop at home.

Anyway things have changed now. Skinner has retired and there's no one to take his place. The last time I saw Barnsley in a cup-tie things were different. They played Manchester United at Barnsley and went down ever so politely 4–0. United played as if they had written the modern theory of the game and Barnsley as if they'd read it backwards. There were no fights either on or off the field, Denis Law shimmered like quicksilver and scored as he pleased, and a young lad called George Best played with the instinctive joy of a genius. There was only one flash of the old fighting spirit. As Law cheekily and magically dribbled round the wing half, stopped, showed him the ball, then beat him again, a bloke standing near us shouted, 'Tha' wouldn't have done that to Skinner, Denis.' Those who remembered smiled. But knowingly.

The Unloved Ones

In the ever-changing game of soccer the lot of the referee remains the same. It is not a happy one. I have always felt sorry for referees, because the job they are expected to carry out is basically impossible.

If they are to do their work properly they have to be able to keep close to the ball throughout the ninety minutes of play, a task calling for colossal stamina. At the same time they are expected to make crucial and often very difficult decisions after chasing 100 yards in even time. Those of you who have run 100 yards in ten seconds, only to be met at the tape by a man from N.O.P. who wants to know what you think about the Common Market, will understand what I mean.

Moreover, the referee has also to contend with the baying of a hostile crowd, the tantrums and snide remarks of the players. And all this for a few bob. Referees know they are not loved except by those nearest and dearest to them. I once saw a referee at Barnsley knocked out by a heavy muddy ball, and as he lay, still and forlorn on the ground and the trainer ran across the pitch towards him, someone shouted, 'Don't revive him, bury the sod.' The rest of the crowd agreed.

The position of the referee in the modern game is probably worse than it has ever been. It is the classic example of responsibility without power. They are continually exhorted to get tougher with the players, and yet when they send off a persistent offender they know that the stiffest sentence the player will receive is a piffling £100 fine and a measly twenty-eight-day suspension.

But whatever happens to improve the lot of the referee, nothing will change his place in society. He will always be unloved by the majority of the population, and will inevitably find it necessary to walk through places like Liverpool with his collar up and his hat brim down, for fear of being recognised. The referee will always occupy that unenviable position of being one who dispenses justice and yet expects none in return.

The saddest example of the referee's plight that I know happened some time ago. His name was Ron and he worked in an office, which fact did not endear him to the majority of the players he was expected to control every Saturday afternoon. Where I lived anyone with a white-collar job was a bit suspect.

Ron was the referee one day in a local Derby game between our village and a team two miles down the road. This was a fixture in which traditionally there was a lot of bloodletting. Rivalries were fierce and a few punch-ups were an accepted part of the event. The two main protagonists were our full back called Blackie and their right winger called Charlie Onions.

Charlie Onions was completely bald and shy about it, so he used to play in a flat cap. The only time he removed his cap was on the odd occasion when he headed a ball and the more frequent occasions when he was involved in a punch-up. During a fight Charlie's cap became a fearsome weapon. He would fold it so that only the peak showed and then use it to belabour his opponent. The moments when Charlie removed his cap in anger were eagerly awaited by his supporters, who would encourage him with cries of 'Gi' him some bloody neb, Charlie'.

Blackie, on the other hand, was quieter, but just as deadly. He was one of those footballers who never said a word, never squealed if you fouled him, but simply awaited the opportunity to get his own back. Always his revenge was swift and terrible. His battles with Charlie Onions were legendary and eagerly anticipated by the crowd.

On the day of the match, Ron, the referee, made it obvious that, tradition or not, he wasn't going to have any monkey business. He warned both Charlie and Blackie that if they started anything he'd send them off.

The game was only five minutes old when Charlie Onions took his cap off to Blackie. Immediately the referee intervened and warned both of them that the next time it happened they would be sent off.

Five minutes later and Charlie again had his cap off to Blackie after a tackle which nearly parted him from his ankles.

The referee raced up to them.

'Off, off,' he shouted.

The two players looked at one another. 'Nay, ref, we're only just warmin' up,' said Charlie.

'Off, off,' said the ref, who was getting very excited.

Blackie said: 'Na' look, ref, me and Charlie don't mean 'owt when we start fightin' and it's what t'crowd expects. So why don't tha' leave us alone?'

The ref was nearly beside himself with frustration and rage. 'Off, off or else I abandon the game,' he shouted.

Blackie looked at Charlie Onions and said, 'Tha' knows, Charlie, I've played this game fifteen years and nivver been sent off, and I've allus said when I do get t'marching orders it will be for summat special. Na', old mate, I don't regard cloggin' thee as being owt special, does tha'?' Charlie shook his head. 'Therefore,' said Blackie, 'I'm about to mek a proper job of things.' Whereupon he turned to the referee and felled him with a colossal right swing.

'Tha's done right,' said Charlie, as he walked off the field with Blackie.

Two weeks later Blackie was in the boozer when they brought the news, Len, the trainer, said to him, 'They've banned thi' *sine die*.'

'Is that bad?' asked Blackie.

'and felled him with a colossal right swing'

'It means for good, that's all,' said Len.

'That's all right then. I wor ready for retirin', any road,' said Blackie.

Blackie didn't suffer. Later that season they held a benefit game for him. The posters advertising the game said, 'Proceeds for a deserving charity', because they couldn't announce they were collecting for a banned player. The referee, on the other hand, got little sympathy from anyone, and eventually went to live in Wakefield.

If you go back to the village now they'll still point Blackie out to you, and tell you how he fixed the referee.

All he did was to express in one massive right-arm swing what anyone who has ever been to a football match has felt at one time or another. We've all nurtured a secret desire to chin the referee. Knowing this, and knowing also that the referee is aware of it too, I am filled with wonderment and amazement every time I see them trot on to the field of play. How many men do you know who would walk into the jaws of Hell knowing that their only reward is a few bob and the scorn of their fellow men?

Christmas at Home

What we used to do for Christmas was share a pig with three or four other families. Throughout the year we would take it in turns to clean and feed it and then, just when we were getting fond of it, my old man and his mates would send for the local gamekeeper who would slaughter anything for a couple of bob and a pint or two. I can remember standing outside the pig sty – a very small child – tears running down my face at the noise of the carnage inside.

One year someone pinched our pig. They waited until it was fattened and ready for the kill and then spirited it away at dead of night. We never found out who it was but ever after we mounted guard on our pig sty from November onwards, protecting it from evil, saving it for the slaughterman.

Our Christmases really began when the pig was jointed, jellied, pied, sausaged, rissoled, trottered and shared out among the owners. Looking back, Christmas to my child's mind was a rich stew of smells and sensations. The table groaned, for the one and only day of the year, under the unexpected weight of food, men I only saw in their working clothes and pit muck turned up in tight blue suits and Co-op shoes and aunties with new hair-do's seemed suddenly aware of what they'd kept under their pinafores all year long, and the air was heavy with Soir de Paris and the promise of sex.

Our Christmases were divided into three main compartments. Eating and drinking, sporting, and partying. We always used to have the parties at our house, not because it was any bigger than the others in the street but because my old man was the unchallenged party giver of the entire South Yorkshire coalfield. Virtually teatotal the year round he broke the rule at Christmas when a pint of bitter mixed with his extraordinary output of adrenalin made him an uproarious and indefatigable host.

In my father's book there were only two categories of people, those who could take a joke and those who couldn't. He loved the former and ignored the latter, although to be fair

142

to the latter, you had to be pretty patient and even-tempered to appreciate some of my father's jokes. For instance his favourite party piece was a game called 'Press it on' which, adapted by father, was sub-titled 'blacking up'.

This involved the unwitting co-operation of one of the guests who was hand-picked each year by father and asked to come to the party only that father might play his joke on him. At a suitable time during the evening, when everyone was well bevvied and burping gently, father would seat his sucker guest on a chair and stand behind him with his back to the coal fire. The other guests would be instructed to form a seated circle alongside the chosen guest.

My old man then explained to the poor sod sitting inno-cently in front of him that the game was a simple one in which my father would touch the guest's face with his finger and the guest then had to duplicate the touch on his neighbour's face, who would pass it on until it came full circle. The trick was, my father explained, to duplicate the touch absolutely and not to laugh. If, in the opinion of the honoured guest, the fellow players did not duplicate the face touching properly and/or he laughed during the proceedings they would be due a forfeit.

What the victim never realised, of course, was that before father touched his face he first of all daubed his fingers with soot from the fireback. Years of practice had confirmed that he could completely black a person's face without the victim knowing a thing providing none of the other guests let on. The moment when the victim was given a mirror and came face to face with the appalling mess my father had created was a real test of his good humour and my father's skill at convincing him that he was now a member of an elite club. I saw him perform his trick on about a score of victims and the only time it went wrong was with the local sanitary inspector who stormed off home and then sent dad a bill for ruining his white shirt. Father stated he never did like the fellow and said that in any case he was the one that pinched the pig.

Looking back, the sharpest memories of Christmas were the football matches. It seemed that in my childhood Barnsley never stopped playing football over Christmas and I never missed a match. Christmas matches were different altogether. In the bus going to the ground the men were wearing new scarves and gloves and they smoked cigars instead of

Woodbines. In the ground the normal smell of stale beer from a lunchtime session was replaced with whisky aroma from a thousand miniature bottles which were produced from inside pockets and offered surreptitiously to the man next door in the way they might proffer a glimpse at a dirty postcard.

Things were different on the field of play, too. The players of my yesteryear were not the mechanical, processed zombies that pass for athletes nowadays. They were flesh and blood characters with a lust for life and not the sort to deny the temptations that inevitably came their way every Christmas. There was one player in particular, a full back of Scottish ancestry, who, in all the Christmas games I saw him play, never gave the slightest indication that he was sober.

I once saw him score twice through his own goal and only be robbed of a hat-trick by a magnificent save from our goalkeeper. On this occasion he was so drunk that when the ball arrived at his feet he simply whacked it away from him in the direction he was facing at the time. If he happened to be pointing towards his own goal then he was in imminent danger of being top scorer for the other team. He was prevented from any further assaults on his own goal by the intervention of our captain who, the next time the full back received the ball, tackled him with great ferocity causing an injury which had the full back being led gratefully from the field. Our skipper was then booked by the referee for fouling a member of his own team and everyone looked bemused about the whole affair.

It was the same player, and a Christmas game, who prepared to take a free kick and, after placing the ball, walked backwards, forgetting that the Barnsley pitch was surrounded by a low wall which protected a drop of about six feet into the terraces. As fifteen thousand spectators and twenty-one colleagues looked on, open mouthed, the full back continued his long march backwards until the back of his knees came into contact with the wall and he toppled into the crowd. The trainer went to have a look at him but he seemed so peaceful and content snoring gently at the feet of some of his greatest fans that he decided to leave him there for the rest of the game.

There was, in fact, great sympathy among the Barnsley crowd for this full back. I think they saw in him their own frailties; he was their reminder of the night before. In fact, he looked like they felt.

Today the players get a bit of time off over Christmas and, in any case, wouldn't dream of disgracing their profession by getting trousered on the field of play. The crowd has changed too. If they produce bottles nowadays it is likely to be for the purpose of breaking it over someone's head rather than sharing a drink with a neighbour. Nor, I'll bet, are there many people at a modern soccer match who share a pig with their neighbours and not a soul, I'll wager, who had his face blacked by my old man.

They are ghosts, now, in my Christmas past.

. . . and Abroad

Christmas games were special. Everything was different. Behind the goals there were more cigars than Woodbines, the bottles of Scotch flickered twixt hip and lips with the lightning speed of a humming bird's wings and the crowd rustled in its new clothes. The players were affected too, they even looked different. As a boy I imagined the change in countenance was due to the fact that they, like the rest of us, were sprinkled with Christmas stardust.

Later, as the layers of naivety slipped from me, I came to know that they were simply hungover. I first came face to face with the truth during a Christmas game some years ago when a full back on Barnsley's side played in the most erratic manner. He appeared to be unsteady on his feet and quite unable to decide which side he was on or what he was supposed to be doing. The truth dawned as he ran to take a free kick, missed the ball completely and fell flat on his back. He lay there for a while, feet and arms feebly twitching, until suddenly he was still and at peace.

The crowd regarded all this curiously and silently for a

'they, like the rest of us, were sprinkled with Christmas stardust'

moment, and then someone yelled: 'Look at 'im, lying there like a roll of bloody lino.' The crowd roared and the trainer grinned sheepishly as he went to work with the smelling salts. Accounting for this unique slice of behaviour an official communiqué, issued some time later, said that the full back had suffered an 'emotional disturbance' before the game and this had affected his play. The old man told me, on the quiet, that the emotional disturbance was caused by the change in the licensing hours at Christmas.

To me as a child Christmas was simply a matter of how many points Barnsley took from their three games. It also meant a new pair of football boots or a shirt from a football-daft father. 'Who are you this year,' he'd ask, as I got all togged up at 5 a.m. on Christmas morning. 'George Robledo,' I'd say, and race out of doors to play a game with my imagination under the flickering gas lamps with the windows in the other houses still dark and sleeping.

In those days I became a new player every Christmas . . . George Robledo, Jackie Milburn, Peter Doherty, Stanley Matthews. And if, during the season, the player whose identity I had assumed fell from grace I would quickly transfer him to another club and pick another player. The day I stopped dreaming was the day I bought my own football boots.

The first Christmas I ever spent away from England was a melancholy one. It was difficult in Africa to make-believe Christmas in Barnsley. We did the next best thing by organising a Boxing Day football match against a team of locals. The opposition played without boots and displayed a weird assortment of skills. I was matched against a lanky and toothsome native who possessed the most staggering ball control. Time and again he dribbled the ball towards me, his toenails glinting like piano keys, and I, full of nostalgia and Army pudding, would watch his feet like a mesmerised mouse, quite unable to do anything sensible or effective.

When he'd had enough of teasing he would slip by me as if I were invisible and as he did so, just rub it in, he'd bellow 'Stanley Bloody Matthews' and laugh triumphantly. This kind of humiliation had gone on for far too long when I was approached by our left full back, a squat, hard little man from Doncaster, who was renowned for his simple and uncompromising attitude towards life and football.

147

'Th'art using wrong tactics against him, sir,' he said.

'Really,' I said, 'and what, pray, do you suggest?'

'He needs cloggin', sir,' the full back said.

'Cloggin'?' I queried, acting dumb.

'Pinnin', clobberin' . . . *stuffin',*' he replied.

I said I got the message. I thought the proposition over. I considered the effect that this new tactic might have on world-wide race relations and wondered further whether or not at Christmas, of all times, I ought to sanction the kind of local war the full back was suggesting. But I was too full of self-pity and misery to care. 'Go ahead. But be gentle,' I said. The full back grinned and moved away to mark the winger. The first time they met the winger showed him the ball and flicked it past him and was away with a derisive shout of 'Stanley Bloody Matthews'. I grinned pityingly at the full back, but I could have spared him any sympathy.

The next round was all his. As the winger moved downfield, the ball dancing at his feet, the full back struck like forked lightning. There was the terrible noise of bone on bone, and a flash of toenails and pink soles as the full back took the winger and the ball over the touchline. After a while the winger opened his eyes and looked dazedly and questioningly about him. The full back, standing arms folded and surveying his handiwork, stared back and answered the question. 'Wilf Bloody Copping,' he explained. It was the only whiff of home I had all that African Christmas.

The best Christmases of all were when we travelled away with Barnsley with the light ale under the seats and the kids on the luggage racks. The men, free from the pits and full of best bitter, filled the compartment with football talk and we kids, wrapped tight in new clothing, sat above them and got drunk on their arguments and their memories.

In those simple daft days nothing was more important than the coming match. We were ruled by a passion that relegated everything, no matter what, to second place. And if Barnsley won we'd speed home on silver wheels with the compartment full of bottle tops and singing. At the station someone would always ask: 'And how've you gone on?' And we'd always say: 'Two points and eight pints of bitter.' When we reached home the old woman would look at the old man as he came through the door and she'd know by his face what had happened.

If he was smiling she'd nip upstairs and get changed and they'd both go off for a Christmas drink at the boozer, leaving me at home to nurse the memories of the day like a hot-water bottle.

Today, of course, it's all changed. This Christmas I didn't see a single football match and somehow I didn't miss it. I worried about it a bit and I looked at my eldest son for signs of reassurance, for some indication that he had inherited the family's football fever.

'How did Chelsea go on today?' I asked.

'Don't know, but I tell you what, Daddy, Batman's being turned into an iced lolly.' His eyes stood out like gobstoppers.

'It's about time Tommy Docherty transferred him,' I said peevishly, and reached out for a bottle of pain-killer.

'"Wilf Bloody Copping," he explained.'

Unlikely Wonders

One of the first things you learn in sport, if you are wise, is never to be put off by appearances.

Not all great soccer players have legs like Bobby Charlton, or foreheads like Tony Hateley. Not all great bowlers have Fred Trueman's shoulders; not all great batsmen Graveney's style. The trouble is that as children we are constantly presented with a picture of the sportsman as superman. This is partly to do with the child's distorted view of life which makes every sportsman ten feet tall even if he happens to be Harry Pilling. (My first traumatic experience occurred the day I discovered I was two inches taller than Skinner Normanton.)

But mainly it is caused by the stuff we read in the comics. When I was a kid I firmly believed that every athlete looked like the Great Wilson, who wore a black vest and Bermuda beach shorts (which in those days were called short long 'uns) and once ran backwards up Everest. I was prepared to accept that not every athlete followed his eccentricities of dress, but I was perfectly convinced that they all had his magnificent physique, his wind-swept good looks and overpowering modesty. Even when Wilson ascended Everest years before Lord Hunt he made little of it.

As I remember it he left his companion in camp at the base of the summit and disappeared, running backwards, into the swirling mists. He returned two days later and when his companion asked him if he had made it, he gave him the kind of look which suggested that he (Wilson) had indeed been where no mortal man had set foot. I believed every word of it even to the extent where I once considered writing to Sydney Wooderson advising him to improve his physique by trying Wilson's diet of wild berries.

Wooderson was probably my first link with the real world of sport as opposed to the comic book version. At first I didn't believe him. He looked like a superannuated bowling-green attendant. Then as childhood fell away and my eyes narrowed

I discovered that he personified one of sports's most exciting and moving sights, the weed who performs wonders.

Tommy Harmer was like this and probably gave me my greatest moments. I saw him once at Old Trafford with Spurs looking like an elf in a forest of oaks. That day he was magical. The ball was his obedient servant, the other players his slaves.

Jimmy Leadbetter who played for Ipswich during Sir Alf Ramsey's great days there had much the same quality as Harmer. It seemed that when he came on the field he wasn't there. But it only took five minutes to discover that it was Leadbetter operating from no-man's-land with his almost apologetic manner, who was both architect and artist to his team.

All of which brings me to Swot, so called because that was what he was. In the swaggering, sports-mad days that the rest of us enjoyed at Grammar School, he was a lonely figure, excused games because of bad feet but 'persuaded' to a weekly humiliation in the gymnasium by a PE master whose idea of assistance over a vaulting horse was a well-placed kick up the backside. I shall never know what finally decided Swot to take up sport. All I do know is that when he asked the sports master if he might be allowed to play in the soccer session none of us could believe it. When he turned up on the field of play he looked like an advert for War on Want. He still wore his rimless swotting specs but was otherwise normally attired except for a pair of hockey pads he had borrowed from his sister which he wore outside his stockings. We asked him where he wanted to play, feeling certain he wouldn't know what to say and were mildly surprised when he said 'Centre-forward, I think.' His opponent, a burly youth called Moggins, put Swot at his ease by saying 'I'll put you out of your misery quickly Swot. You won't know what hit you.'

But it didn't happen like that. Swot in fact scored four goals and revealed quite staggering ball control. Afterwards he confessed that he had decided to learn the game from a book and had practised at home. He was at present immersed in C. B. Fry and thought that he might soon be ready to play cricket.

When the season changed Swot played his first game and scored a lovely thirty-odd, basing his technique solely on Fry's dictum: 'Play back or drive.' Swot's place in our society improved in direct relationship to his increasing prowess at games. He was no longer chided and teased, and even the PE master showed his approval by rationing himself to only one kick at Swot's backside during the gymnasium session.

Soon Swot became brave enough to bend our ears with his theories on sport. He said that sporting ability was a clear-cut example of mind over matter. Anyone with a brain could learn to play a game reasonably well, and one's ability increased in direct proportion to the size of one's intelligence. That being the case, he said there was every reason why the best scholars should also be the best sportsmen, providing they applied themselves and given always that they didn't have one leg or something.

This theory was too much for the likes of the unfortunate Moggins, who was under no doubt that the reverse was true and could prove it by comparing his dismal academic career with his prowess at games.

Eventually the conflict was resolved when Swot asked Moggins how they could put their theories to the test. 'Boxing,' said Moggins. We tried to talk Swot out of it but he wouldn't listen. He locked himself away with several books on the ancient and noble game and finally emerged saying he was prepared.

In the ring he struck a stance, left foot forward and bent at the knee, which suggested the books he had learnt from were several decades out of date. Moggins, several inches taller and two stones heavier, sneered once and then destroyed all Swot's theory with a roundhouse right which would have demolished a concrete air-raid shelter.

Swot was never the same after that. He went back to his books and his solitude and Moggins once more strutted the school, having proved to the rest of us that sport was a triumph of brawn over brain.

I didn't quite feel that way and found no solace in Wilson, and the rest of the sporting heroes in the comics. Now it was they and not Swot who seemed ridiculous. Looking back I can now see that Swot was an important figure in my sporting life. The sire to a new delight.

Success

In fact, I never wanted to be successful. I simply wanted to be famous. The kind of fame I had in mind as a child was the kind given in Yorkshire to the one who wears the white rose on his cricket cap. More reverence than fame, I suppose. In my imaginings I didn't bother dreaming of making a century for Yorkshire, I concentrated on what it must be like to have peple recognise you in the street and point at your house. Little did I know it but it was good training for the future.

Similarly as a junior reporter on a local newspaper in South Yorkshire my sole ambition was to have my name above the story. The story wasn't important, the recognition that I had written it was everything.

One day the editor called me into his office and briefed me on my first by-line story. It was, he explained, 'the biggest society wedding the South Yorkshire coalfield has ever seen'. This seemed to me at the time a contradiction in terms, but I didn't argue.

Reporting a wedding for a local paper is merely a matter of getting the names right and this time I made doubly sure, checking and re-checking the list. I sent my copy off to head office and waited up overnight for the result to be shoved through my letterbox. For the first time I was about to see my name above a story. Came the morning and I opened the paper with the nervousness of a playwright after a West End opening night. There, on the front page, was my masterpiece and above it, my name. I read the article with misty eyes and everything was as I had written it until I came to the last paragraph, which read: 'At the end of the ceremony the happy couple exchanged presents. The bride presented the groom with a pair of cuff-links, the groom presented the bride with an electric cock.'

No journalist to whom I tell this story believes it, but I can prove it because in the style-book of that South Yorkshire paper to this very day is the memo the editor sent round all the staff. It said: 'In future clocks, electric or otherwise, will be referred to as "timepieces".' Whenever I consider the past and contemplate my success, as I have been asked to do now, I bring myself down to earth with the observation that after 30 years as a journalist the only footprint I have left in the landscape of my craft is that I changed the vocabulary of one local paper.

If there is a key to being successful then it must be single-mindedness. The objectives can be very different: wealth, power, social standing, sexual conquest, fame or a combination of all of them. But the motive is the fuel and no one of my acquaintance became successful by chance. Nor, in my view, does luck have anything to do with success. The British love to take the view that success is a bedmate of happenstance. In truth – like the old definition of genius – it's a combination of inspiration and perspiration.

In my case the only inspirational thought I had was that in journalism, as in life, one thing leads to another but the chances of exciting exploration are considerably lessened by staying too long in any one place. Therefore, I decided at a very early stage in my career to take whatever work was offered without ever pondering my suitability for the job.

Thus, after a blissfully happy time on the *Manchester Guardian* where I reported everything from chip pan fires in Bolton to Labour Party conferences, I joined the *Daily Express* and became the worst foreign correspondent in the history of journalism when they sent me to the Congo. I slept in the bath to lessen the likelihood of death by a stray bullet and lived on a diet of United Nation's Press Cards which I ate whenever we were stopped at a road block.

This important self-discovery of fear and incompetence under fire would have convinced the normally sane young man that his future lay in the safer havens of journalism. Which does nothing to explain how, some time later, I came to be arrested as a spy in Zanzibar while working for *World in Action*, nor how I found myself surrounded by smouldering armour in the Six Day War trying to report the action for *24 Hours* while, at the same time, writing a column about the golden days of Barnsley Football Club for the *Sunday Times*. When I finally handed in my column to the Israeli censor I was once more nearly arrested for subversive activity on the grounds that 'Ay up' and 'Ee by Gum' were clearly code words defining important military installations.

The importance of all this madness was that it convinced me that I should explore my inadequacies further. Fame was still the spur and gradually I achieved that ambition to the point where nowadays I am rung up by newspapers wanting to know if I (a) sleep in the nude (b) believe in the male menopause (c) have anxiety dreams (d) would have a Corgi as a pet.

Moreover, I receive correspondence from people who are convinced that should I but place my hands on their brow they will be cured of migraine and others who tell me that every time they see me on television they want to throw up. I once had a series of letters from an old lady who said she saw her dead husband sitting next to me on every show and could I ask him to wave now and then, and another from a woman who became so friendly that she sent me a coloured photograph of a scar from her recent abdominal operation.

Such is fame, and the question is, has it all been worth it? Leaving aside the obvious financial rewards, which are high but not as astronomical as the Press would have you believe, the answer is yes and no. For me the great advantage of success and fame has been the way in which it has enabled me to indulge most of those fantasies we all nurture but rarely get the opportunity to fullfil. Thus, not only have I met and talked with Cagney, Astaire, Kelly, Richardson, Olivier, Gielgud, Fonda, Wilder, Lemmon, Matthau, Nureyev, Ali, Betjeman *et al*, I have also played cricket at Lord's, sat in the cockpit of a 747, sung a duet with Bing Crosby, boxed three rounds with Joe Frazier, played piano with Oscar Peterson and appeared in concert with a Symphony Orchestra.

This last fantasy filled me with the most dread. I was asked to narrate *Peter and the Wolf* at the Albert Hall. My fear was based on the fact that although I love music and had always dreamed of standing in front of a large orchestra, I cannot read a score. I met the conductor in a rehearsal room the day before my concert début.

'There is one problem, sir,' I said to him.

'What is it?' he enquired.

'I don't read music,' I blurted. He looked at me patiently.

'Don't worry. I do,' he said.

The problem with success in Britain is that, on the whole, people don't admire you for it. The great curiosity towards it is not how it has been achieved but how it might be explained in terms of luck, birthright, education, double dealing or marrying the boss's daughter. This is not so much an egalitarian theory of life as a doctrine of the humdrum and it is one invented and briskly stirred by my fellow journalists.

No matter. I wouldn't swap my life for theirs. I know, because I've been there. And would I have had it differently? I doubt it. I might have written more but then, there is still time. The problem with an article like this is that it has a valedictory air about it, a feeling that what has been achieved is the summing up of ambition. Not a bit of it. The driving force which aids success might fade but never disappears.

My biggest success has been that never once in 30 years as a hack have I ever wanted to stay in bed unable to face the day ahead. Moreover, I believe I am much the same person I ever was in spite of the fact that my fellow hacks would have you believe that success and fame on television immediately transform you into some sort of monster.

In any case there is always someone who knows to give you advice when you are going off the rails. Just before he died I was talking to my father about this and that and he said, 'You've done well, lad, and I'm proud of you.' Then he paused. 'But, it's not like playing cricket for Yorkshire, is it?' He knew the difference between fame and reverence, success and immortality.